My Dear Departed Past

To Access 21 Original Frishberg Tracks visit
www.halleonard.com/mylibrary

4186-6664-0190-4448

My Dear
Departed Past

Dave Frishberg

Backbeat
Books

An Imprint of Hal Leonard LLC

Published in 2017 by Backbeat Books
An Imprint of Hal Leonard LLC
7777 West Bluemound Road
Milwaukee, WI 53213

Trade Book Division Editorial Offices
33 Plymouth St., Montclair, NJ 07042

Printed in the United States of America

Book design by Michael Kellner

Library of Congress Cataloging-in-Publication Data
Names: Frishberg, Dave.
Title: My dear departed past / Dave Frishberg.
Description: Montclair, NJ : Backbeat Books, 2017. | Includes index.
Identifiers: LCCN 2016043576 | ISBN 9781495071300 (hardcover)
Subjects: LCSH: Frishberg, Dave. | Pianists--United States--Biography. | Jazz
  musicians--United States--Biography. | Composers--United States--Biography.
Classification: LCC ML417.F77 A3 2017 | DDC 781.65092 [B] --dc23
LC record available at https://lccn.loc.gov/2016043576

www.backbeatbooks.com

Contents

Foreword   *vii*

Preface   *xi*

1. **The Dear Departed Past**   1

2. **Do You Miss New York?**   33

3. **Peel Me a Grape**   75

4. **I Want to Be a Sideman**   105

5. **Too Long in L.A.**   115

6. **Dear Bix**   149

7. **Schoolhouse Rock**   153

8. **The Hopi Way**   163

9. **Van Lingle Mungo**   169

10. **Matty**   177

11. **You Are There**   189

12. **Portland**   193

Acknowledgments   195

Index   197

Foreword

Dave Frishberg is a master of nostalgia. Even some of his songs that have no evident nostalgic theme—"Oklahoma Toad," for instance, or "I'm Hip"—manage to envelop the listener in a cloud of reminiscence. Frishberg can't help it. Wistfulness is in his DNA. That is apparent in his piano playing as well as in his writing. He was the perfect pianist for duets with Jim Goodwin (1944–2009), a cornetist equally influenced by Louis Armstrong and Bix Beiderbecke.

Yes, Frishberg is a traditionalist, but he long ago established that he was also in tune with the bebop revolution led by Charlie Parker and Dizzy Gillespie. He was exactly the right pianist for saxophonist Warren Rand's collection of pieces by quintessential bop composer Tadd Dameron. When in the early 1970s trumpeter Al Porcino formed the New York big band that he called the Band of the Century, Dave was the group's first-call pianist. He related with equal effectiveness to the established big-band colleagues whom Porcino recruited and to the eccentric bassist Malcolm Cecil, who went on to found the experimental synthesizer group Tonto's Expanding Head Band.

At twenty-four (after two years in the Air Force), in 1957, Dave moved to New York from his native St. Paul, Minnesota, to pursue a jazz career. He quickly found one. Before long, he was working with Ben Webster, Gene Krupa, Carmen McRae, and Eddie Condon. He joined the Al Cohn-Zoot Sims quartet for extended work at the Half Note, one of the city's prime jazz spots. Let's just say that early on, Frishberg was a mainstream jazz pianist of skill and stylistic flexibility. In a 1970 *Down Beat* review of Zoot Sims and his quartet at Economy Hall in New Orleans, I wrote of Dave's solo on Fats Waller's "Jitterbug Waltz":

> Frishberg evoked the stride era in a couple of opening choruses,
> then settled down to develop some of the rhythmic possibilities of
> ¾ time, building and releasing tension, turning the time around
> and making judicious use of space; all with finely honed humor.

Long loved by fellow musicians and his fans, Frishberg's songs began making their way into the consciousness of wider audiences. In the late 1960s and early 1970s, only the most culturally isolated Americans would fail to recognize the lyric "When it was hip to be hep, I was hep" or the song "Van Lingle Mungo," whose lyric consists solely of the names of vintage major league baseball players. A decade later, "Dodger Blue," a sort-of sequel to "Van Lingle Mungo," became a theme song for the Los Angeles Dodgers, a prominent part of Frishberg's *Retromania* album, and something of a hit for singer Sue Raney. I know few lawyers who don't cherish the lyric of "My Attorney Bernie"—"When he says we sue, we sue. When he says we sign, we sign."

Dave brings his wit and sensitivity not just to lyrics for his own songs, but to the creation of words for music by others. He has provided lyrics to music by Johnny Mandel (the exquisite "You Are There"), Alan Broadbent, Gerry Mulligan, Zoot Sims, and Bob Brookmeyer.

After several years in the Los Angeles jazz and studio milieus, in 1986 Dave moved to Portland, Oregon. He and his wife, April, live in a spacious old house in one of the city's prime residential areas. His custom-built Fandrich grand piano dominates the living room. Now that Portland is their mutual home base, he and singer Rebecca Kilgore continue their frequent collaborations in clubs and recording studios.

Dave can look back on a long and satisfying career, and if he decides that he needs a vacation, he may consider—where else?—Zanzibar.

> You should know before you start, you're about to lose your heart on
> the golden sands of Zanzibar.*

—Doug Ramsey

Doug Ramsey is a winner of the Lifetime Achievement Award of the Jazz Journalists Association. He is the author of the award-winning biography *Take Five: The Public and Private Lives of Paul Desmond* and the novel *Poodie James*. He blogs about jazz and other matters at *Rifftides*, www.dougramsey.com.

---

* © 1984, Dave Frishberg

Preface

THIS BOOK IS A MEMOIR I have written about my life, my early influences, how I became a professional musician and a songwriter, and my life in jazz.

When I was a child in St. Paul, Minnesota, during the Jewish holidays, storytelling was a big part of those gatherings. I loved hearing the stories told by family members and it sparked my imagination and my desire to tell stories too.

In grade school, my neighborhood friend Ron Simon and I made up stories as we walked to and from Groveland Park Elementary School. We invented an adult character named Lemuel C. Lemuel, who was the hero of our stories. Lemuel's adventures often occupied us for days at a time.

My brother Mort taught me to play boogie-woogie and the blues on the living room piano, guiding my taste in music with his record collection. He hooked me on the music that would turn out to be my life's work.

In high school, as a self-taught pianist, I began to make connections with people from different neighborhoods who played instruments and who knew about jazz. To learn the stories about these jazz musicians and their musical world, I started reading *Down Beat* and *Metronome* instead of the *Sporting News* and the *Baseball Digest*.

Stories continued to be a part of my life at college. Without classical training I was not eligible to be a music major at the University of Minnesota. Instead, I was a journalism major and enjoyed interviewing people, learning their stories, and seeing my articles in print. But I did take a number of music-related classes, and I began to meet musicians and started playing gigs.

After graduation, I joined the air force as part of my obligation to the Reserve Officers' Training Corps (ROTC) and was stationed in a recruitment office in Salt Lake City, Utah. My job was writing stories about local soldiers to entice others to join the military. I started writing jingles for commercials and played jazz piano most nights in the clubs and hung out with many of the local musicians. As soon as I completed my two-year service I was off to New York, where I became a professional musician and began writing songs where I could express stories through music and lyrics.

Being witness to the fascinating characters, culture, and events during jazz's golden age, I hope in these pages to share with my readers and my sons, Harry and Max, the rich and exciting experiences I've had as a jazz musician and songwriter.

My Dear Departed Past

One

The Dear Departed Past

The Dear Departed Past

Am I hopelessly old fashioned
'Cause I'm harboring a passion for the olden days?
Is my sense of time so out of joint
It's starting to distort my point of view?

Does my antiquarian brain contain
Imaginary memories of golden days?
Can one feel a real nostalgia
For a time and place one never even knew?

I anticipate times to come with something less than jubilation,
And I'm looking to times gone by with something more and more
Like admiration

Here's to the dear departed past . . .
The musty magazines, the sepia-tinted scenes
Of long-forgotten places.

Here's to the dear departed past . . .
The photographs you find that seem to bring to mind
Familiar family faces.

That's when every sky was bluer.
Clouds seemed to disappear back then.
That's when every friend was truer.
Ah, but then again, didn't they know you when?

Here's to the folks who lived next door.
Let's cut across the yard, drop in and leave a card
With neighborly affection.

Here's to the ways we'll see no more,
The manner and the style that makes you want to smile
In happy retrospection.

As for me, I'll forget about the future,
'Cause the future fades away too fast.
Now's the time to lift a cup of cheer and say, "Hear! Hear!"
For the dear departed past.

Here's to the sides we used to spin . . .
The Deccas and Savoys with all the surface noise,
The Lindy Hops and foxtrots.

Here's to the Orphan Annie pin,
The secret squadron ring the mailman used to bring
For a quarter and some box tops.

Music on the uke was easy . . .
E seventh always went to A.
Chinese checkers and Parcheesi,
And every Saturday, the movie matinee.

I loved the '55 Bel Air,
The '37 fords, complete with running boards,
And rumble seats and fenders.

Where are the clothes we used to wear?
Now don't forget your tie, and button up your fly,
And fasten your suspenders.

As for me, I don't think about tomorrow,
'Cause tomorrow wasn't built to last.
Now's the time to weep a little tear into your beer
For the dear departed past.

While the gang is changing channels
I prefer to comb the annals of the sporting scene.
The biographies and photographs
Of yesterday's athletically inclined.

Though I'm occasionally enchanted
By the sports we take for granted on the TV screen,
Still I get a lot of static
From the sentimental attic of my mind.

And I long for the single wing.
I miss the dropkick and the spitter.
I ignore the expansion teams,
And I deplore the designated hitter.

Three cheers for the champs of yesterday:
Jack Dempsey, John McGraw, Joe Louis, Sammy Baugh,
The movers and the shakers.

And here's to the teams that moved away
From disenfranchised towns: the old Saint Louis Browns,
The Minneapolis Lakers.

That's when basketballs had laces,
And halfbacks played safety on defense.
That's when there were parking places,
A hot dog for a dime, White Castle seven cents.

And here's to White Castles by the sack.
I heard somebody say they're still around today,
But they wouldn't taste the same now.

Here's to the years that won't be back.
The days that dodged away, and left us here to play
A completely different game now.

And here's to the echoes of tomorrow,
Soon to be memories at last.
Mem'ries that will someday reappear loud and clear
In the dear departed past.

Words and music by Dave Frishberg
© 1982 Swiftwater Music

Reminiscing

"Am I hopelessly old-fashioned 'cause I'm harboring a passion for the olden days?"

Let's say I have a near-pathological involvement with the past—the twentieth century in particular. The song "The Dear Departed Past" deals with this disorder, which I imagine might be commonly referred to as "memory worship" or "hubba-hubba syndrome."

Reminiscing? Oh yeah, I'm an expert. I can even reminisce about the word *reminisce*, as follows: In the summer of 1963 in New York, soon after I had joined Ben Webster's quartet, Ben was at the microphone introducing the next song, "Danny Boy," and he turned to me at the piano and said, "Reminisce."

I said, "What?"

He said, "Reminisce."

I said, "What are you talking about?"

He said, "While I'm talking to the people, you reminisce behind me."

Then I understood and began to play soft chords as he spoke to the audience. Now whenever I hear a piano player doing that, I say to myself, "Reminiscing."

"Is my sense of time so out of joint it's starting to distort my point of view?"

Absolutely. Somebody once called my attention to this fact. My wife and I were sightseeing in London, and I was getting bored. We strolled by the Tate Gallery, and I stopped and said, "This is the bench! This is the spot! Come over and sit here."

My wife said, "What for?"

"Because this is where Dick Thompson and I sat in 1952. Ironic, isn't it, that we should be sitting here on this bench. This is the very spot. And you remember what he said, don't you? I must have told you a dozen times. This is where Thompson said he didn't know whether—"

She interrupted me. "I see. You don't experience anything while it's actually going on, do you?

"Life becomes real for you only when you can reminisce about it."

Bull's-eye.

"Here's to the ways we'll see no more. The manner and the style . . ."

Duke Ellington, who had both the manner and the style, said it more concisely: "Things Ain't What They Used to Be." But retromaniacs like me can't leave it at that. No, I have to keep grabbing your sleeve and pointing out what took place sixty years ago, and urging you to take another look, give another listen. When I inspect my catalog of songs that spans about fifty years, I have to gulp when I realize that maybe 50 percent of the lyrics are concerned with The Past, and what a drag it is that The Past is no more.

"Can one feel a real nostalgia for a time and place one never even knew?"
Are you kidding? I'm nostalgic about stuff that hasn't even happened yet. Once I was asked to write a TV production number about Earth Day to be sung by multiple voices. I decided to write what I considered a science-fiction song—an anthem to be sung five thousand years from now on a distant planet where humanlike creatures will join hands like paper dolls, proclaim they are descended from earthlings, and promise never to forget it. I finished the song, and days passed before I realized that I had only fallen again into the same old pit. What do Frishberg's people do in the future? Why, they reminisce of course. To my credit, though, I had sense enough to restrain these humanoids from chanting ballplayers' names. And speaking of sports . . .

"I ignore the expansion teams, and I deplore the designated hitter."
It's true, I don't pay much attention to anything that happened in sports after about 1950. If you asked me what teams played in last year's World Series, I'd have to think it over, because chances are I don't remember.

"That's when basketballs had laces."
Right, and the baseball players I reminisce about wore wool uniforms with pants rolled at the knees. They used to leave their gloves on the outfield grass between innings. In those days, big-league ballplayers made so little money that even the biggest stars had to work off-season jobs to make ends meet. Those ballplayers were like musicians! Don't

you get it? Because they chose to follow their passions! Pardon me for shouting, but for some reason this all seemed heroic to me then, not to mention romantic. Hey, I was fourteen years old.

From the time I was seven years old I had been making pencil drawings from photographs in newspapers and magazines showing athletes in action and in posed portraits capturing their facial expressions and body language. I felt I wanted to make a career as a sports illustrator, but my obsession began to fade when my brother Mort introduced me to listening and playing music.

A Step Above Organ Grinder

In St. Paul during the years of World War II I was attending grade school, and Mort, seven years my senior, was finishing high school. Our older brother Arnold was on a tanker in the South Pacific. If I had a question about music or anything else, I naturally went to Mort, who was my adviser and authority about everything. He guided my reading toward Ellery Queen, Dorothy Sayers, Robert Benchley, and James Thurber, and focused my attention on the best movies, magazines, and radio shows. We listened to *Vic and Sade* every day.

We would listen to music carefully and somewhat analytically. In what we called the sunroom was a big Philco console that contained a record changer. Alone, I would sample the record collection for hours, sorting through the heavy albums filled with single 78s, staring at the labels: Decca, Bluebird, Vocalion, Okeh. My brother Arnold's collection was big-band-oriented with Benny Goodman, Artie Shaw, Cab Calloway, and Count Basie heavily represented. But Frankie Carle was in there, too, along with Kay Kyser and Raymond Scott and Horace Heidt. There were many titles by Bing Crosby, and several by Ella Fitzgerald and Mildred Bailey. I could sing along with all of them. My specialty was singing songs by Gilbert and Sullivan, especially the entire score of *The Mikado*. I read along with the libretto, but most of it I could do from memory.

By the time Mort was at the University of Minnesota, he had become a blues and jazz aficionado and undertook to guide me about the music and the players. He collected piano records, especially blues and boogie-woogie. Albert Ammons, Pete Johnson, and Meade Lux Lewis, of course, but also the more obscure players, like Jimmy Yancey and Pine Top Smith. Mort was crazy about Art Tatum, Teddy Wilson, Jess Stacy, and Mel Powell. Those were the piano players I listened to carefully as a young boy. Count Basie's playing charmed me too, as did Jelly Roll Morton's special touch and deep time feel.

Mort was also deep into folk music and played for me the records of Woody Guthrie, Leadbelly, Cisco Houston, and Josh White. He could strum a guitar well enough to perform this stuff in a fairly authentic way, and together we could sing an odd eclectic repertoire learned from records and radio, including "Rock Island Line," "Goodnight Irene," some cowboy songs like "Old Shep" and "Red River Valley," and religious songs like "Dust on the Bible" and "(I've Got My) One-Way Ticket to the Sky."

Mort had lost interest in piano lessons, but he could play by ear. His repertoire was pretty well limited to the blues, which he learned off the records. He knew how to play the blues piano licks, keeping a strong rhythm and slurring off the black keys. He showed me how the blues was structured—twelve measures divided into three groups of four bars each. I understood quickly, and I began to play the blues, copying Albert Ammons and Pete Johnson. They each had their characteristic bass figures, and I worked hard to get them under my left hand, striving for strength and steadiness of beat. I tried to get that skipping buoyancy that those players had, but that was the hard part, where they showed their real finesse. I learned the recordings chorus by chorus and tried to copy as exactly as I could. That was very important to me as a young player—to try and duplicate what I heard, and make it as accurate as possible.

I was beginning high school by this time. Mort had gone into the navy, and I divided my home time between three main activities: making pencil drawings of athletes in action (I copied these from photographs), pitching a tennis ball against the front steps, and playing boogie-woogie on the piano. My social life at Central High was stretching out too, because I was meeting a lot of new people from different neighborhoods, and among these new acquaintances were some kids who played instruments and actually knew about jazz musicians like Charlie Ventura and Dizzy Gillespie. Instead of *Baseball Digest* and the *Sporting News*, I was now buying copies of *Down Beat* and *Metronome* and wondering who these new musicians were and how their music sounded.

When I got hold of Mezz Mezzrow's book *Really the Blues*, which had recently been published, my musical imagination was fired, and I began to search through the household record collection for specimens by Mezz's friends and colleagues. At Louise's Music Store in downtown St. Paul, I made my first record purchase—a Brunswick album of 1928 Chicago jazz by Frank Teschemacher, Jimmy McPartland, Bud Freeman, and the other early "hepcats." Mezzrow's book made such a strong impression on me that I accepted everything he had to say without question, and therefore considered his music and his opinions to be the gospel of real jazz, and everything else to be "commercial," hence shallow and unworthy of serious attention. My friends at school suffered my disdainful comments about the music they listened to: "Stan Kenton! That's commercial crap! You ought to be listening to Sidney Bechet and Muggsy Spanier." At age fifteen I was a stodgy purist, following the gospel of Mezz, which led to the smug and comfortable notion that "modern," or "progressive," music—or "sounds," as they called it—was not jazz at all, because, not being related to New Orleans jazz, it was not authentic.

Leo Adelman worked one Christmas season at my dad's clothing store. He was a few years older than I and had a reputation around town as a hot trumpet player. We chatted one day about music. I was raving about my favorite trumpet players, Muggsy Spanier and Wild Bill Davison, and Adelman fixed me with a puzzled eye. "I dig Red Rodney," he said. I had never heard of Red Rodney, and before I knew it, Adelman was explaining how modern musicians played extensions off the chords—"changes," as he called them. I told him I had heard the Dial record of "Ornithology" by Charlie Parker and was puzzled because I didn't understand the song. "Why, it's nothing but 'How High the Moon,'" he explained. That evening I played the record, and, as if the sun had broken out of the clouds, I understood in a stroke what Adelman was talking about. It was a deciding moment, because I comprehended for the first time the infrastructure embodied in composed music, and how the jazz improvisers were honoring it in their own highly stylized way. Unlike Mezz, they weren't interested in keeping the tradition pure. They wanted to put their individual personal touches on the songs and comment on the music by tampering with the harmony. The audience they were playing to was made up of other musicians, and it was like an inside joke, plus a chance to demonstrate their jazz credentials, show how musically adroit and sophisticated they were. I was fascinated, and I wanted to learn all about Parker and Gillespie and the musical game plan that they and the other young players had embarked on.

Mort was working at the Roycraft Company in Minneapolis, administering the Columbia Records distributorship. During the Christmas rush one year I worked a few days in the Roycraft shipping room, filling orders for Columbia albums and singles, fetching the stock from the shelves and stuffing the packages for shipment. Also working part-time as a shipping clerk was Jimmy Mulcrone, a sallow guy in his mid-twenties who was active as a bebop pianist in local nightclubs. We talked about music, and I played him the boogie-woogie records I had made at Schmitt Music. "You can play," Mulcrone said. "But I can show you some things."

For the next few months I traveled for my music lesson each Saturday morning by bus and two streetcars to where Jimmy was living, in Northeast Minneapolis. He wasn't exactly giving me piano lessons, because I wasn't learning exercises and classical technique. What Jimmy offered to show me was how to use the piano to deal with music—music theory, essentially, or keyboard harmony. Since the blues was the only song form I had ever dealt with at the piano, I knew how to build seventh chords on the degrees of the scale I recognized as one, four, and five. Jimmy quickly showed me how to incorporate a new chord—what he termed the "two" chord—into the blues framework. "It's called a minor seventh chord," Jimmy said. And as Jimmy demonstrated the voicings of the minor seventh chord and how it behaved as an auxiliary to the related five chord, I was stunned by sudden insights and revelations that would shape the rest of my life. The systematic magic and mathematics of music were being revealed to me, and I was blown away by the power and logic of it all.

I recognized notes on the staff, but I couldn't read them and execute them quickly. Struggling through piano notation was such an unrewarding process that I lost patience with it. The music died when I tried to read it. Mulcrone saw that I was a natural player, and he didn't try to teach me songs with sheet music. Instead he made lead sheets—just the melody with chord symbols—and I could quickly make sense out of those. The early songs he assigned me were

"Just You, Just Me," "Lover Come Back to Me," "Body and Soul," and "What Is This Thing Called Love," including its then popular bebop treatment called "Hothouse." "Body and Soul" was a challenge because of the five flats in the key signature. He showed me how to play "Robbin's Nest," and I recognized the minor sevenths and understood how they worked. He wrote out "Elevation" so I could see how the beboppers treated the blues form. It all made perfect sense to me, and I began to listen voraciously to the new music. I was under the spell of bebop.

What Mulcrone showed me during those Saturday mornings was enough to keep me subsequently occupied for years, sitting at the keyboard discovering how to navigate music by using music theory as an expressive tool: essentially, how to speak the language of music, how to fake—*fake* being a non-opprobrious term meaning "to play solo or in an ensemble without written music." The ability to fake on your instrument was essential to getting employment at nearly any level of the music business, especially in the world of swing and dance bands. Jazz musicians were among the best fakers of course, and some raised extemporaneous playing to artistic heights. But faking was no big deal for a professional sideman, and neither was improvising; there was nothing remarkable about using these rudimentary musical skills. By showing me how to deal with music analytically, Mulcrone gave me my first glimpse into the secret world of jazz musicians, magic people who could casually play songs in any key, who talked about "chord changes," and whose repertoire was seemingly limitless. Jazz musicians were hip, they were funny, they were sensitive, they were clannish, and they seemed to have the best girlfriends. I liked being around jazz players, and I wanted to be one of them.

It's important to remember that this jazz musician dream-life had nothing remotely to do with money or fame. That's because the music business—they didn't call it an "industry" then—held little promise for that kind of success. There was no career path to a jackpot in the music business. There seemed to be a goal, and that was to play good music in the big leagues, with good musicians. The path to that goal was to get good enough on your instrument, and then learn the professional skills, including faking, reading and writing music, transposing, stylistics, improvising, and repertoire. Then you would begin to get gigs. The process would lead you to play better and better, and it followed that you would get better gigs, and "better gigs" didn't always pay better money. "Better gigs" meant that you were playing with better musicians. If that involved better remuneration, then that was just luck. Sure you might get lucky, but that was another story. As the saying went, you were more likely to make a killing than to make a living. To have all this pleasure plus make a living would be nothing short of a miracle.

What's the alternative? Trying to sell something? No thanks. What are the pitfalls? You might have to play bad music, but probably not forever. Alcohol, drugs, nightlife, women? Hey, I can handle that. I want to play with Stan Getz, I want to hang with Peggy Lee, I want to be in Woody's band, I want to sound like Jimmy Rowles, I want to sound like Horace Silver. I want to play in the big leagues. It was a clear trade-off: You choose music, you say goodbye to financial security and a predictable future. This was the same choice you'd face if you were deciding to become a professional ballplayer—another career that didn't pay off in cash in those days. My parents listened to my pianistics with puzzled disapproval, and I once overheard my dad telling his friends that I wanted to be a "klezmer." I could hear him shrugging with disappointment. In his mind, a dance band musician was a low performer, a clown, maybe a step above organ-grinder.

1950s Hipster, Junior Grade

Howard's Steakhouse was a nightclub on Olson Highway in north Minneapolis. On Sunday afternoons there was always a jam session at Howard's, featuring the two tenor saxists Chet Christopher and Oscar Frazier. My ex-mentor Jimmy Mulcrone was the piano player, and he invited me to drop by any Sunday and play. My pal Myles Spicer borrowed his dad's Studebaker one Sunday and the two of us showed up at Howard's at three o'clock, right on time for the music. This must have been around 1949 and would make me sixteen. I looked even younger, obviously too young to be in a bar. Mulcrone came to our assistance and assured the boss that we kids were there to hear the music, and we got a ringside table and sipped Cokes.

Here's what I remember about the band at Howard's: Norm Nelson was on bass, Jimmy Mulcrone on piano, Pat Fitzgerald on drums, Frazier and Christopher on saxes, and Ira Pettiford on trumpet. Among the sitters-in were Maurice Talley, conga; Don Specht on piano and trumpet; Jerry Trestman, Bob Crea, and Ray Komischke on sax; and Sheldon Rockler (of the Minneapolis Symphony Orchestra) on trumpet. Mulcrone beckoned me to play, and I sat at the piano. Chet Christopher asked me if I knew "Red Top," a blues in F, and I was happy to answer yes. I don't remember much about the experience except that I loved it and wanted to go back to Howard's every week. I returned once or twice, but I soon got the message that youngsters were not really welcome.

Now in my junior year at Central High, I had met Harold Gillman, who played clarinet and saxophone and listened to Charlie Parker records. We got together with Dick Kohn and Leon Katz, both drummers, and Bob Shadur on trumpet, and had a session at Shirley Kaplan's house on Lincoln Avenue. Jerry Paymar, Myles Spicer, Ted Birnberg, and Adrian Warren were there too, as listeners. Shirley's house became headquarters for after-school hanging out, and I played a lot of songs at the big upright piano. Shirley used to sing "I've Got News for You" and "June Comes Around Every Year," which she had learned from Woody Herman records.

Harold Gillman came up with my first paid job: He put together a band to play a dance at the gym at Marshall High School in St. Paul. Harold played clarinet and alto sax; Charles Meyerding played trumpet; Tom Tjornhom played trombone; Conway Villars was the drummer; and Sumner Benson was the bass player. The singer was Chuck Williams. I think we faked most of the tunes, but there was some reading involved—stock arrangements and lead sheets. Chuck Williams sang in a Billy Eckstine style, and I remember he sang "Don't Blame Me" and "Without a Song," among other standards. Harold handed me $12 after the job. I loved every minute of it.

Tom Tjornhom recommended me for the piano chair in Bob Ochs combo, a much more polished group than Harold's pickup band. Ochs's band played parties and school dances and worked several times a month. Bob was a senior at St. Thomas Academy. He played trumpet and wrote the arrangements. King Jobson from the U of M was usually the drummer; Bob Jensen from Roosevelt High in Minneapolis played bass; Tjornhom, who attended Northwestern College of Chiropractic, played trombone; and Paul Finley, a med student at the U, played tenor sax. The piano chair had been covered by a phenomenal pianist named Tom Coller, who was off to Catholic seminary to study for the priesthood. Coller played serious classical piano at a very high artistic level, performing Rachmaninoff concertos and impossible Liszt and Busoni pieces in concert.

I auditioned by faking "September in the Rain" in E-flat. Bob Ochs said, "You got the job." "I'm a very slow reader," I warned him. Bob said, "Take the piano parts home and learn them." "I can't do what

Coller does," I said. Bob assured me that it wouldn't be necessary. I couldn't wait to get home and dive into the piano book.

The piano parts were laboriously copied two-staff piano accompaniments with no melody cues. This meant that I had no idea what the lead melody sounded like or what the band was playing. Since most of the pieces were original compositions by Bob or jazz tunes I had never heard of, the Bob Ochs piano book was a total mystery to me. So I got busy and began to decipher every measure. To my horror, many of the parts were without chord symbols. Bob apparently wasn't a fan of repeat signs or ditto marks, so each part folded out into eight or ten pages. "The Peanut Vendor" was twelve pages long, and consisted of the same figure repeated again and again for twelve pages. I read each measure carefully to make sure that all the measures were identical in every respect. I called Ochs and said, "'The Peanut Vendor' is the same figure one hundred and thirty-six times. Why not just once with a repeat sign?" "Tom Coller wrote that part," Bob explained. I told him, "Tom's going to make a great monk." Ochs and I became good friends and the combo had quite a few gigs.

During that summer of 1949, the Bob Ochs Combo drove up to northern Minnesota and camped in tents in a trailer park near the Ochs family summer vacation home in Park Rapids. Bob had actually booked a couple of afternoon gigs for us—one in a small restaurant in Nevis, and another in Walker, where we played in a giant tent that was used for big revival meetings. We set up on the dirt floor and began to play our bebop songs. Admission was twenty-five cents, and we had only one customer all day. He was from the nearby Indian reservation, dressed in feathered regalia with bells on his ankles. He wore moccasins and stepped quietly around in the dirt, doing a shuffling jangling dance. He danced on and on while we played "Elevation," "Hothouse," "Over the Rainbow," and our theme song, Charlie Ventura's "High on an Open Mike." Whatever tempo we struck, he just kept on shuffling and jangling at his own pace. Our drummer, Conway Villars, shouted out, "He's marching to a different tom-tom!" and we all broke up. Today when I hear "Elevation," the classic Gerry Mulligan piece for the 1948 Elliot Lawrence Band, I still think of that American Indian in Walker, Minnesota.

Being in a band was as exciting and rewarding as I imagined it to be. Word got around that I could play, and I began to meet a whole new cast of characters and discovered that I needed to be versatile and quick so I could fit into any kind of band and, as often as not, play piano parts that I had never seen in situations I had never considered.

One of my first gigs with real professional players was subbing one night at the Midway Gardens on University Avenue in St. Paul. The drummer, Elliot Fine, was the leader, and we had to play for a roller-skating act. Elliot yelled, "Temptation!"; the bass player yelled, "C!"; and we were off, with the sax playing lead. I loved it. At the bridge I had the melody. Talk about faking. Later the drummer yelled, "Offenbach!" and everybody began to play the Barcarolle from *Gaîeté Parisienne*. The male skater clamped his jaws around a leather belt and began to spin his partner, who was hanging by her teeth on the other end, in giant circles parallel to the floor. They came nearer and nearer the piano until her skates were whistling WHIFF WHIFF WHIFF so close to my face I began cringing down around the bass notes. Later I told Elliot I better buy an insurance policy to do this work, and he said to be sure and get the roller-skate rider.

One night I went to play the first set at the Jolly Miller Room at the Nicollet Hotel in Minneapolis. The piano player was going to be a half hour late. The leader was Cecil Golly, ("Music by Golly"), and he was not pleased to see me. Nor was I pleased to confront the stack of piano parts that loomed before me. Reading was not my bag. Sight-reading stock arrangements without chord symbols was for me a matter of listening to what everybody was doing and trying to do something appropriate while counting the measures. The bass notes were often helpful. On this occasion there were brass, woodwinds, and strings in the band, so I wasn't carrying the lead and was able to lurk and listen. The theme song was "Linger Awhile," which I had heard on radio broadcasts from the Jolly Miller Room. So I knew about the bell tone between the notes *ling* and *ger*, and as the set began and we played the theme I rang it out precisely each time. Mr. Golly, as I probably called him, said "Very nice." After that I could do no wrong.

But mostly the gigs were jazz jobs, because that was the popular music of the time, and at nightclubs or dances or wedding parties, or in movies or on the radio, it was likely you were hearing music generated by dance band instruments: saxes, trombones, and trumpets and acoustic basses, lots of piano, and singers (I don't remember calling them vocalists), who were most often not the headliners. Strings were still important, but beginning to vanish from the landscape. Amplified guitars had not yet overwhelmed the industry and transformed our culture, and pianos were practically everywhere. Even the cowboy band on the WDGY Barn Dance had a piano.

When I got to the University of Minnesota in the spring of 1951 (after a couple of quarters at Stanford University in California), I began to play jam session concerts at the student union with other young jazz players I had met on campus. Among them were bassists Dick Thompson and Ted Hughart; drummers Jack Cottrell and Shelly Goldfus; trumpeters Dick Zemlin, Jack Coan, and Glenn Baxter; and the saxophonist Dave Karr, who turned everyone around with his brilliant playing and musicianship.

Karr's presence in the ensemble made all of us sound and play better. Dave had recently arrived from New York City and enrolled at the U of M. He was a year or two older than us, maybe twenty-two or twenty-three, and had some professional experience with name bands; he knew a lot of the big-league cats and had played with them in New York. Along with Al Cohn, Zoot Sims, Alan Broadbent, Bob Dorough, and a handful of others, Dave Karr must be included in my list of the most gifted musicians I ever ran across. Among them, both Cohn and Karr were profoundly influential on my life and music, and I felt privileged to know them and count them as friends.

Because I was under twenty-one, I really couldn't spend too much time in nightclubs, which is what I was itching to do. When jazz acts would come to town and play at the Club Carnival or Vic's in Minneapolis or the Flame in St. Paul, my friends and I would sometimes just hang around outside, digging the music that leaked out, and sometimes catching a glimpse of the musicians, maybe even having a chat. When Louis Armstrong played the Carnival, we lurked around by the parking lot and got to chat with Earl Hines and Barney Bigard. I can't remember what was said, but I know we were trying to be as hip and cool as we could be. We were hipsters, after all. We knew about tag endings and coda signs.

Bob Crea and Bob Kunin, two excellent saxophonists, were working all the time in jazz clubs, and through them we met some big-time players who would hit town for a week or two, long enough to shake everybody up. We met and got to sit in with Conte Candoli, Serge Chaloff, Charlie Ventura, and Lou Levy. Our friend Don Specht was playing piano with the house quartet at the Flame. We'd hang around to say hello to him on intermissions, and we got to hear and see some of the big acts that played the Flame: Billie Holiday, Ella Fitzgerald, Charlie Ventura's band with Jackie Cain and Roy Kral, and Johnny Hodges's band with Lawrence Brown and Sonny Greer.

It was through Specht that I played my first nightclub jazz job. He asked me to sub for him at the Flame for two or three nights when he had to miss the first set. I was especially thrilled to get this call, because Art Tatum was the headliner that week. Tatum had John Collins on guitar and Slam Stewart on bass. One thing I noticed while watching Tatum for a few nights was that he could play the same piano arrangement in different keys if he wanted to, and the two sidemen were cracking up trying to outguess where Tatum might go next. I went home fairly early each night because I had school the next morning and homework to do. When I closed my eyes I would see a piano keyboard, and I'd drift off to sleep that way, not hearing the music, but visualizing the voicings on the keyboard.

On Sunday afternoons, the jazz players and their chums, wives, and girlfriends would gather at the Hoop-de-Doo, a joint on lower Nicollet in Minneapolis. The pianist Bob Davis ran the jam session there. I got to play with the hip local drummers like Bill Blakkestad, Mel Leifman, and Russ Moore. Ted Hughart, Norm Nelson, and Dick Thompson were among the bass players. Other pianists I remember were Don Specht, Bob McCaffrey, Rufus Webster, and Lou Levy. Jack Coan was among the trumpet players. The saxophonists Karr, Kunin, and Crea were regulars. Traveling musicians were off on Sunday, and they would hang at the Hoop-de-Doo.

It was during those days that I first experimented with marijuana. Everybody at the Hoop-de-Doo was getting high on something or other. Pot was popular with just about everybody, and I noticed that the heroin users clanned together in little groups and talked in secrets. I was not interested in sticking a needle into my arm for any reason, but I was a cigarette smoker big-time, so inhaling something illegal for a thrill was no problem. Hey, let's light up and be like Mezz and the boys! Someone slipped a reefer into my hand, and presently Dick Thompson and I stood in a parking area behind the

Hoop-de-Doo, nervously puffing and holding our breath. I became dizzy in a benign way, laughed hysterically as we walked around the block, and then went back up on the bandstand and announced to the other players, "Hey, this is great!, and I really feel like playing!" Then I played as if in a trance, completely tuned in to the sounds around me, and playing with instincts and discriminations that I had never been in touch with. I loved it. Then when it was my turn to solo I forgot what song we were playing, and I couldn't continue. Someone hollered out the name of the tune, and I resumed. But now I was beginning to sweat with anxiety, feeling sure that narc agents were noting my every move, and my heart began to pound at the prospect of going to jail. One customer spoke to another at the bar; I was positive the guy was talking about me and the reefer. He had spotted me and Thompson smoking in the parking lot! I was sure of it. In a panic, I left the piano abruptly and fled into the men's room and flushed away the rest of the cursed cigarette of evil. I was paranoid and distracted the rest of the afternoon. Thompson seemed quiet and absent, but he was often that way. On the way home we discussed buying some pot. Now we knew where to get it. I could hardly sleep that night, thinking of how close I had come to total disaster—a life sentence in prison. But I was hip.

Aaron Copland?

In 1952–53, while a student at the University of Minnesota, I shopped around for a couple of years, trying to decide what I wanted to study. At Stanford I had begun to prepare for a major in psychology, so I continued with that, but I wasn't much interested. I was mainly concerned with staying out of the draft for the Korean War and hanging around Scott Hall, where all the music students were. In order to be a music major you had to be an instrumentalist, and I, an "ear" pianist with no classical repertoire, could not present the required senior recital. So I enrolled in all the music courses I was eligible for, which included theory, music history, and other non-piano classes.

I was eager to learn about how to write for the various instruments, mainly the reeds and brass, so I could make jazz arrangements. I enrolled in a class called Introduction to Orchestration, taught by composer and choral director James Aliferis. I was distressed when I found out that we wouldn't hear our orchestrations played. We handed in our scores, and Dr. Aliferis would examine them on paper, note any mistakes and point out difficult or impossible passages, and inform us that certain doublings or registers would not sound good when played. I said, "It would be great if we could hear what we've written."

He replied, "Of course. But composers and arrangers don't have that luxury. They've never had it. Occasionally we'll assemble some musicians to play the outstanding student orchestrations, but for the most part we'll be dealing with the score on paper."

We started with strings, and I chose to orchestrate elementary piano pieces that I was familiar with, although I couldn't play them. Dr. Aliferis was unimpressed with my string charts, graded them accordingly, and scolded me. "Surely you can find something a little more challenging to work with, Mr. Frishberg. We're going to study woodwinds now, and I suggest you investigate some piano pieces by Ravel, Debussy, the more contemporary literature."

Seizing the opportunity to deal with something I was familiar with, I selected a jazz piece by Al Cohn called "Four and One Moore" and arranged it for five saxophones. Dr. Aliferis handed it back to me marked F. "Saxophones? We're not writing for a dance band here. And where's the original piano score? And please find some music that's more interesting than this. Have you investigated Scriabin? Saint-Saens?"

Of course I had investigated nothing of the sort. I was just trying to deal with music I was vaguely familiar with. Scriabin? Who was that? Now, faced with the next assignment—brass instruments—I decided to just grab a sheet of modern piano music at random and, without hearing it played, just assign the notes willy-nilly to the various instruments, and let the chips fall where they might.

In the library I pawed through piano folios of contemporary composers and came up with Béla Bartók's *Mikrokosmos* and selected one of the pieces near the back of the book, a piece where the notation appeared more complex and difficult. It was called Romanian Dance Number Three or Number Four—something like that, and it was four pages with a lot of notes and an odd time signature. I had no idea what this music sounded like; was it supposed to be fast? Slow? Is this line supposed to be the melody? I just mechanically wrote down the notes and found there were six voices to be assigned. I arbitrarily decided to make them two trumpets, two trombones, and two French horns. At a certain spot, just for the hell of it, I specified mutes for one trumpet and one trombone, and other than that, I gave no thought to register, breathing, or phrasing. How could I? I couldn't even imagine how any of this was supposed to sound. It was just notes. What if this passage is impossible to play on the trombone? Aliferis would catch that error, and what was the difference, because it would never be played anyway. I handed in my score, and when he saw the title Dr. Aliferis glanced up at me with a surprised look.

When I returned to orchestration class a few days later, Dr. Aliferis made an earnest announcement: "Mr. Frishberg has handed in one of the most extraordinary pieces of work I've seen this year. I'm pleased to inform you that you'll be able to hear this piece next week, when musicians from the Minneapolis Symphony Orchestra will play through some student compositions and orchestrations. Congratulations, Mr.

Frishberg. Here's your score"—it was marked A-plus—"and please prepare parts for the six musicians. We'll run through your Bartók piece first. I would say it's not more than two minutes long. Is that about right?"

My heart was pounding as I absorbed the impact of this news. I choked out a reply, "Yes, that's about right."

I showed up at the rehearsal a week later and passed out the parts, depositing the score on the conductor's music stand. Aliferis was there, along with my six brass players and Gerard Samuel, an associate conductor of the symphony. Dr Aliferis introduced me to the players, stepped aside, and handed me a baton. My knees buckled. I stared at the musicians and they were staring at me. "I'm afraid I don't know how to conduct. I don't know how to begin." The truth was that Bartók's piece was a total mystery to me; I couldn't begin to play it, literally could not count the first measure with its Greek time signature. I didn't have a clue what that music was supposed to sound like on the piano, let alone with a mixed brass ensemble.

Gerard Samuel came to my rescue and, taking command without the baton, briskly swept the six brassmen into the music, and they were off, as I listened with my mouth open. The music was jerky and rhythmic, with eccentric accents and intervals, and it was neatly executed. Before I knew it, it was over—it had lasted maybe a minute and a half. Mr. Samuel made some suggestions, and the musicians made some pencil marks, and they ran through it again. I was speechless and amazed because the orchestration sounded good. Thanks to sheer luck I had blundered into a comfortably playable arrangement of the Bartók piece. I was laughing to myself at how preposterous this was. A deaf person could have done what I did.

The musicians turned to other material and I excused myself with profuse thanks to everyone. Dr. Aliferis drew me aside and introduced me to the man standing with him—Aaron Copland. Copland was visiting the university, speaking that afternoon at the Student Hour in Scott Hall. I knew of Copland, of course, but I wasn't familiar with his music, and here he was complimenting me—"I love your Bartók transcription."

After all that, I found myself a few days later back in Aliferis's class, still clueless about orchestration. Now I had to pull off the next assignment—writing for piano, harp, and percussion—and I still hadn't any idea what I was doing. That might have been when I decided to try the School of Journalism.

(And when I think of Aaron Copland, I'm reminded of the following incident related to me by singer Pinky Winters: During the 1970s, the L.A. Philharmonic presented Benny Goodman playing Aaron Copland's clarinet concerto. The Goodman band was featured first, and Pinky was backstage digging the music from the wings. Standing near her was Aaron Copland, and they exchanged polite greetings.

The band was wailing and guitarist George Benson was taking an extended solo. Copland's ears perked up. He couldn't see the stage and he asked Pinky, "What is that instrument I'm hearing?"

Pinky responded, "Why that's a guitar."

"No, no! I mean the solo instrument," said Copland.

"It's a guitar," Pinky said, "an electric guitar with an amplifier."

Copland was astonished and said, "What will they think of next?")

Serving My Country 1955–'57

In the spring of 1955, soon after I graduated from the U of M, my ROTC agreement required that I begin active military duty. The air force assigned me to a recruiting detachment headquartered at Fort Douglas, an antique Union Army post in the hills of Salt Lake City.

How did I wind up in the air force recruiting business? Simple.

My college profile showed that I had a degree in journalism, as did numerous other young lieutenants arriving in that graduating class. The armed services were all in the process of demobilizing, getting rid of personnel, and demoting highly paid career officers down to master sergeant rank. What to do with all the educated "journalist" lieutenants they suddenly found themselves with? They decided to make us into "public information officers," feeding newspapers pictures and stories about the local kids who had recently joined the air force, making sure all the recruiting sergeants had the latest posters and propaganda, delivering air force radio and TV programs to stations, and arranging special "flyovers" and other ceremonies for holidays and state and county fairs.

The work was fussy and boring, but I got to leave the office every day and hang out with reporters and announcers and disc jockeys. There were weekly routine reports and other correspondence, and after I got the hang of it, the work was easily accomplished by noon on Monday, and I would sign out on the office blackboard each morning, often naming my destination as "Manila" or "Winnipeg" or whatever.

Our commanding officer was Major Edward Michael, an ace bomber pilot over Germany, who was awarded the Congressional Medal of Honor for his gallant accomplishment, returning a crippled and burning B-17 back to England, across the English Channel, thereby saving the lives of four crew members.

Major Michael took a liking to me, and he understood why I was uncomfortable with being a military guy. He was uncomfortable himself, because the air force had declared him unsuited to fly jets. He had been traumatized and emotionally scarred by his ordeal in the war. The air force permitted him to fly prop planes, and he kept his flying career alive with weekend flights with C-47s, but his heart was broken when he couldn't qualify for jet pilot. He was miserable and restless with his recruiting duties; he wasn't remotely interested in sitting behind a desk.

My desk-mates in the large main room were all master sergeants and staff sergeants, all grizzled vets, military career guys with combat experience in World War II and Korea. To them, this recruiting duty was a posh assignment, with special comforts and advantages. They resented me and made no secret of it from the moment I walked in the door in my ill-fitting summer uniform. I upset these guys in many ways: I was a college boy, I was Jewish, I was a commissioned officer with no military experience, I had lucked into a simple two-year tour of duty, and did I mention I was Jewish? They were really upset that they had to call me "sir" and salute me. I didn't blame them, but I didn't like them, either. By the end of the two-year episode, our relationship had become congenial, and I had become a first lieutenant.

Scatman

I used to visit Idaho—Twin Falls, Pocatello, and Idaho Falls—when I was stationed in Salt Lake City with the air force from 1955 to 1957. I once played in Twin Falls —are you ready?—Scatman Crothers. He must have been down on his luck at the time, playing in a tiny cocktail lounge, accompanying himself at the piano. I was in town for a day or two on air force business—in uniform—and was bold enough to sit in, as I knew his repertoire of standards and jive tunes. He played brushes on snare drum. We had a great time, and I came back the next night. We were cookin'! About thirty years later Scatman had become newly famous as an actor. I ran into him in L.A., and mentioned the Twin Falls episode. He looked at me as if I were from Mars.

Birdland in Utah

There were no living quarters at the fort, and all the personnel lived off-post. The air force subsidized me $75 per month for off-post rent, and I was able to find an apartment pretty easily at that price. My monthly pay as a second lieutenant was $232. I lived comfortably, within my means, and even managed to make monthly payments on my '55 Chevy Bel Air. I remember that my grocery budget was informally set at $10 per week.

I found a two-room furnished cottage in a forested neighborhood not far from Fort Douglas. It was called Allen Park Drive and Bird Sanctuary. Allen Park was picturesque in a seedy way. A brook ran through the premises, and there were several stone footbridges that led to the cottages along the edge of the forest. Birds were everywhere—in the trees and waddling all around the grounds. Driving along the gravel road to the bridges, one would pass the exotic birds that were kept in big cages. These imprisoned birds would call to me as I arrived and departed each day. The talking mynah bird at the main entrance would croak, "Hello, soldier!" and, "Bye, soldier!" I figured out that the bird would use this greeting when he saw a man drive by wearing a hat. The remarkable part is that the bird would recognize a departure from an arrival, and change his line accordingly. All female drivers and hatless males would get only "Hi!" in either direction.

Checking for mail each day at the reception desk in the main cottage, I would be greeted with cold grunts from my landlord, Dr. George Allen, a white-haired sixtyish gent, who often peered out from a room where I could see him working with a printing press and stacks of pamphlets and flyers. I asked him one day what he was printing back there, and he handed me a sample copy of a tabloid-size newsletter called *The Pheasant Gazette*.

Dr. Allen's potato-like wife sunned her feet in the driveway during summer days, and I would sometimes see her sitting barefoot in the passenger seat of her car chain-smoking Kools with the door open.

She gave special attention to her ankles, trying to warm them in the sunshine: with a cigarette dangling from her mouth, she would smear them with ointment. Like her husband, she didn't have a whole lot to say.

The cottages were styled like log cabins. Mine had a tiny bedroom and bathroom that looked out onto the forest in back. I played my Woody Herman, Stan Getz, and Charlie Parker records loudly whenever I was home. I didn't really care who heard them. I read a lot of books and wrote a lot of letters. At night I would haunt the nightclubs and hang with musicians. As the summer of 1955 waned and the nights got chilly, I would turn the electric heaters on, and my bedroom was pleasantly warm. I slept soundly, unaware that the forest animals were now starting to seek seasonal cozy quarters for themselves. My pillow was next to a large open pipe—five or six inches in diameter—that jutted out from the wall near my ear. The pipe was stuffed tightly with wadded newspapers, and I hadn't paid any attention to it.

I heard a scratching sound one night so close to my ear that I woke up terrified. An animal was tearing and chewing madly at the paper inside the pipe. It was, to judge from the frenzied gnawing sounds, a husky rodent with little patience or self-control. I leaped into my clothes and walked briskly down the path to the main office. The birds in the cages woke up and began screeching and cawing. When Dr. Allen answered the doorbell in his printer's apron I could see that he was busy in the shop and *Pheasant Gazette*s were spinning out of the press at full speed. Since it was about four in the morning, I was relieved that at least I hadn't awakened him, but I thought it was strange that he should be up printing at this hour.

Mrs. Allen appeared in a robe and slippers. It was the first time I had seen her wearing foot covering of any sort. Dr. Allen explained to her, "He says there's an animal trying to get in through that vent pipe."

I told him, "Bring a long wire so you can stick it up the pipe." Dr. Allen paused for a puzzled moment, then said, "We won't need that," and the three of us trudged silently up the path to my cottage.

When we got into the bedroom all was quiet inside the pipe. Dr. Allen said to his wife, "I don't hear anything, do you?" Then he started pulling the wadded paper out of the pipe. "STOP!" I hollered and grabbed his arm. "What if he comes out into the room?"

Dr. Allen told me to get a paper bag. I fetched a grocery bag from the kitchenette. Dr. Allen pulled out the rest of the paper and peered into the tube. "I can't see anything in there. It's probably a wood rat, but he's gone now." The sound of the words *wood rat* sent chills up my spine. "Poke something up there. Make sure he's gone," I begged, and then I stared in horror as Mrs. Allen stuck her arm right up the pipe. "There ain't nothin' there," she said. Dr. Allen began to stuff the paper back into the pipe. I flattened my back and palms against the wall behind me and said to Dr. Allen, "Maybe he's pressed himself against the inside of the pipe so you can't reach him—like this, you see?" Dr. and Mrs. Allen stared coldly as I demonstrated how a rodent might conceal itself. Then they left the cottage without further comment and strolled back up the dark path past the shrieking inhabitants of the cages that lined it.

I had trouble sleeping there after that, sometimes reading 'til dawn, always on the alert for the dreaded scratching. My problem was solved about a week later when I got orders to go to Lackland Air Force Base in San Antonio for a nine-week recruiting training course. I packed up as fast as I could and checked out of Allen Park Drive. The mynah bird duly acknowledged my departure.

When I returned to Salt Lake nine weeks later, I rented a cheery one-bedroom apartment on Barbara Place, about a mile west of the fort, and that became my home for a year and a half.

Finally, in 1975, I was in Salt Lake City traveling with the Herb Alpert band. I rented a car and took my pal the percussionist Julius Wechter for a biographical tour of the city—"Here's my bank. Here's where I took my laundry, here's where I bought groceries," and so on. I found the renamed street that once was Allen Park Drive, and Julius and I were astounded to come upon a white-haired hag sunning her feet in the driveway. Julius said, "Is this the Bird Lady?" I called to her, "Are you Mrs. Allen?" She said yes, and we had a short conversation. She said, "No more birds. Too much trouble since Dr. Allen died in 1960. Got a couple birds in the house. Don't remember anything about a wood rat. Nope. No vacancies."

Julius liked to tell the story of the Bird Lady of Salt Lake City. Years later I thought of a good line but never got a chance to drop it on Julius, who by that time had died.

Two

Do You Miss New York?

Do You Miss New York?

Since I took a left and moved out to the coast,
From time to time I find myself engrossed
With other erstwhile denizens of the Apple.

While we sit around and take L.A. to task
There's a question someone's bound to ask
And with this complex question we must grapple.

Do you miss New York? The anger, the action?
Does this laid-back lifestyle lack a certain satisfaction?
Do you ever burn to pack up and return to the thick of it?
Or are you really sick of it, like you always say?

Do you miss the pace? The rat race, the racket?
And if you had to face it now, do you still think you could hack it?
When you're back in town for a quick look around, how is it?
Does it seem like home or just another nice place to visit?
And were those halcyon days just a youthful phase you outgrew?
Tell me, do you miss New York?
Do you miss New York?

Do you miss the strain? The traffic, the tension?
Do you view your new terrain with a touch of condescension?
On this quiet street is it really as sweet as it seems out here?
Do you dream your dreams out here? Or is that passé?

Do you miss the scene? The frenzy, the faces?
And did you trade the whole parade for a pair of parking places?
If you had the choice, would you still choose to do it all again?
Are you sitting in front of the tube, watching Annie Hall again?
And do you ever run into that guy who used to be you?
Tell me, do you miss New York?
Me too . . . me too.

Words and music by Dave Frishberg
© 1980 Swiftwater Music. All rights reserved.

My Shot at the Straight Life

When my military obligation was nearing fulfillment, I still had a couple weeks of leave time I hadn't used. I decided to fly to New York to get a job. At Major Michael's suggestion, I traveled in uniform at no cost on military planes. I checked into a hotel in Times Square, bought a *New York Times*, went straight to the classified ads, and began calling employment agencies. I was scouting around for a songwriting job largely with ad agencies and jingle producers. Within a day I had landed a job writing "continuity" material for WNEW, a big New York radio station. My job would begin in two weeks. I hurried back to Salt Lake and began to disassemble my life. I was excited as hell.

They signed me out of the air force in June 1957 at Hill AFB in Ogden, Utah, and I practically flew out the gate, drove back to Salt Lake City, packed my records, books, and clothes into the Chevy Bel Air. I was off to New York to start my job in a couple weeks at a radio station, and to be where the music action was, and maybe get to play with some of the guys I admired on records.

I didn't stop home in St. Paul this time, just drove madly across the country, impatient to get to the Apple and my new life. Popping green Dexamyls, my heart pounding with excitement, my head swimming with ideas, I composed songs out loud as I pounded the beat on the dashboard.

When I got to New York I drove to the Upper West Side and checked into the Paris Hotel for $9 a night. My room was cramped and without a bathroom, but I was accustomed to bunking and flopping in strange places and on friends' floors, and I didn't care about comfort. I called the only New Yorker I knew. It was Bob Pincus, whom I had met in Salt Lake City when he was Corporal Pincus. Now he commuted every day from Long Island to his job on Park Avenue. I announced that I was in town, scheduled to start my new job in a couple of days.

"Get rid of your car," he commanded. "You won't need a car anymore. Park it in the garage on 96th and West End, and I'll arrange to have it sold." The next day I parked my beloved blue Bel Air at the garage and hopped a cab to Rumplemayer's, where Pincus was waiting. He bought me a drink and we discussed our plans to share an apartment. Pincus and another guy from Great Neck wanted a place to stay in town a couple nights a week and they offered to pay two-thirds of the rent for that privilege. Together we pored over the classified ads and Pincus evaluated the prospects by address. He wanted a prestigious address, said that was important for his work.

"Besides," he explained, "you meet a better class of people."

Within a few days I sublet a big apartment at 1 West 64th, on the corner of Central Park West, and Pincus was delighted by my choice. The rent was $200 a month, and Pincus and his friend Ray Lapof agreed to chip in $60 apiece. A Metropolitan Opera singer by the name of Henry Cordy was the permanent tenant of the eight-room monster apartment. My eyes popped when I saw the big grand piano. Mr. Cordy locked up the rear areas of the apartment so that we were left with four rooms to roam around in for the next six months. Neither Pincus nor Lapof spent much time at our luxurious midtown pad, so I was content to be alone with my exciting new life. I was in New York and I had a job.

At home in my spacious sublet I played the piano furiously at all hours. The grand old building had thick walls and ceilings, and I never heard a peep from adjacent neighbors. But one guy could hear me across the courtyard and he would holler, "Take a break, fa Chrissake!" I wailed on with my mad bebop. It didn't bother me that I was disturbing someone else. I remember clearly my attitude in 1957: I am at large in New York City, and if I feel like playing the piano at midnight, I don't care who might be listening or what they might think. In other words—I could hardly contain myself.

~

I began working at the station in early July of 1957. WNEW was New York City's most prominent radio station. The studios and offices occupied the entire second floor of an elegant office building that overlooked Fifth Avenue at 46th Street. The sound of WNEW was "sophisticated" cutting-edge pop music, stuff that today might be classified adult easy listening. "N-E-W," as New Yorkers referred to it, had the most popular and influential disc jockeys playing hit songs around the clock for a loyal audience that numbered in the millions. Art Ford and William B. Williams had the top-rated music shows. *Milkman's Matinee* ruled the nighttime hours, and Gene Klavan and Dee Finch's loony morning show was a breakfast habit of a lot of New Yorkers. It was said of William B. Williams that he was "the Sinatra of disc jockeys," and it was he who named Frank Sinatra "Chairman of the Board."

The walk from my apartment near Columbus Circle to the WNEW studios was an easy one, and each morning after breakfast at a drug-store counter near the Mayflower Hotel, I would hike briskly to work, clutching my *New York Herald Tribune*, which I had quickly adopted as my favorite paper. The uniform of the day was a suit and tie.

My job was called that of "continuity writer," and it paid $65 a week. The announcers and disk jockeys were responsible for reading scripted copy from the big logbooks that the producers placed in front of the microphone. The scripts included commercial copy, noncommercial spot announcements, and "continuity" announcements, which were often just a sentence or two, like "Stay tuned for Lonnie Starr right after the news," or "Want to be Sinatra's guest at Frank's opening in Vegas? Details on *Klavan and Finch* tomorrow morning."

Bill Persky was the head of continuity, and his pal Sam Denoff was head writer and my supervisor. They had been in the continuity department for two years when I arrived, and Persky had just been made boss and Denoff had slid up a notch, leaving the staff writer's post vacant. An employment agency had sent me over there to interview for the job, and Persky and Denoff both gave thumbs-up on me. "Now, you're not going to run off and join a band or something, right?" Persky had asked, only half joking. I could see he was uneasy, because he sensed that I was crazy about making music. I really wanted the job, though. Partly because I thought they were the hippest and funniest guys I had ever met, but mainly because I felt working at WNEW would put me in touch somehow with the music business, and I had a vague idea that eventually I might even do something musical at the station, like maybe produce a live music show.

My job was mainly writing copy for NCSAs—noncommercial spot announcements. The commercials were written and supplied by ad agencies, but the noncommercial, or "public service," spots most often had to be written in our office. The spots were for government agencies or nonprofit organizations such as the Red Cross, the United Negro College Fund, Hofstra College extension courses, Catholic Charities, the U.S. Coast Guard, and so forth. There was a mountain of promotional pamphlets, newsletters, handouts, and brochures on my desk, and I had filing cabinets full of the stuff. For each public service "account," I would compose three spot announcements: a sixty-second, a thirty-second, and a ten-second station ID. I had to update the copy for each account, and the task had been neglected for months. I got involved in it and put a lot of thought and energy into transforming the raw copy, which was often lifeless and unfocused, into punchy scripts that would sound good on the air. Besides that routine, Denoff and I would dream up station promotions and stunts, and I was excited to watch from behind the glass while New York professional radio actors performed my scripts and skits.

Persky and Denoff stayed late every night, sometimes working into the morning hours, churning out scripts for television comedy shows. They hadn't had much luck yet, but they had already connected with Carl Reiner and Sheldon Leonard, and were only a few years away from hitting it big in L.A. with *The Dick Van Dyke Show*. They both loved to laugh, as did I, and we all found the same things funny. Denoff was always "on," and the announcers would tell him he should be on the air, not them.

One morning in August, Gene Klavan and Dee Finch, the early morning madcap announcer team, had joined us in the continuity office to listen to Sam hold forth. Denoff was reading the paper out loud. Sam said, "Look, the Russians are building an earth satellite just like we are. But the Russians are hip. They have names for their space-craft: *Sputnik*, *Luna*. We should have a name for our earth satellite. Why don't you guys run a contest on the morning show? 'Name the Earth Satellite.' Winner gets a trip around the world. We'll get Wernher Von Braun, Willy Ley, and maybe a couple of generals to be the judges. They'll select the winning name. We'll screen the entries, of course, and we'll send the scientists five or six names to choose from." Klavan's eyebrows went up. "*We'll* screen them? Who's 'we'?" And all eyes swiveled to where I was sitting. Denoff stood up and announced, "Davy, you're gonna go through the mail each day and pick out the likely candidates."

The "Name the Earth Satellite" contest lasted about a month. Mail sacks filled with postcards were delivered to my desk, and I inspected several hundred cards every day and tried to select plausible and appropriate satellite names. My eyes were popping out of my head. There were hundreds of *Stargazer*s and *Wanderer*s, of course. It was also plain to see that a significant percentage of the contestants were pretty well bonkers—their entries ranging from bewildering non sequiturs to incoherent scribbling, unreadable graffiti, and delusional ravings. I started setting aside the bizarre entries and the pile soon grew. Typical specimens:

> *My suggestion is* Roscoe. *Simply because it's daring, catchy, different, and impish.*

> *I suggest we call our earth satellite* CANCER *for the following reason: "Cancer"—the Crab. Dimmest of the Zodiac.*

> PREABO BLAFLRE. *Why: It is a mnemonic for*

PRE-ATOMIC BOMB BLAST FLIGHT REFUGE
So if you're small you could get out of it with your skin.

Please name the earth satellite testis. *This is a*
Latin word meaning "eyewitness."

Greetings: The name of the earth satellite should
be Keep New York Clean, *to honor the campaign*
to keep our great city clean.

I think NEOTARSHI *is appropriate. It is an original*
word comprising letters most often occurring in terms
describing weather conditions which the satellite
will predict.

Name the earth satellite SWEN. *Its letters contain*
those of WNEW; stand for South, West, East, and North;
and spelled backwards it's NEWS. Suggest it be
pronounced in swift low resonant tones as "Swennnn."

Name: The Pope
Reason: Because it's capable of so much good.

One woman from Brooklyn wrote a long message each day, proposing a new name each time. Each name was a crazed reference to teeth, chewing, or dental procedures "I think we should call the earth satellite *Autoclave*, because they sterilize dental instruments used in fixing teeth." or "Why not call the earth satellite *Gum Decay?*"

Why not indeed?

I don't remember what was chosen finally for the satellite name.

Denoff, Persky, and I would go through each day's selections, with Sam usually taking over as reader, using a loud, droning, Ed Sullivan–like delivery. Station personnel passing the continuity office in late afternoon would gather to witness the three of us howling and weeping, falling to our knees, pounding on the walls, so helpless and convulsed with laughter that on several occasions I was afraid I was going to lose consciousness.

~

WNEW was the last New York radio station and probably the last in America to employ a full-time band. Accordionist Roy Ross was the leader, and the band played for the daily Bob Haymes show, which went from noon to two. The musicians arrived at the studio at 9 a.m., the same time I reported for work. My office was across the hall from the big studio where they did the Haymes show. I would hear the band rehearsing the day's arrangements every time the big soundproof door opened and shut, and I would often drop in and watch them deal with the new music. I marveled at their reading skills, and I admired the neat little arrangements they would play. Of course I let it be known that I was a piano player, and they were absently unimpressed. Walter Iooss, the bass player, made pleasant conversation with me each day. One morning, after writing all night at Cordy's big grand, I brought in an arrangement of "You're Getting to Be a Habit with Me" and asked Walter if the band would play it. He frowned when he looked at the bass part. "That's not really the bass line," he said. "Unless you get the bass line right, the whole song sounds wrong." Then he showed me at the piano what the bass line really was, and I understood why that was necessary to make the song sound like the composer intended. It was a breakthrough moment for me, something

I kept in mind as I started to think analytically about the composition of pop songs. I was relieved then that the band didn't run my chart, because I would have been embarrassed.

I began to spend all my coffee breaks watching the band rehearse, and often would just hang around smoking a cigarette, digging the rehearsal and wishing I were involved making music instead of just watching. Hal Moore, the program director, had to come one morning and escort me back across the hall to my desk. "You're spending an awful lot of time with the band. Are you sure you're not going to walk out of here and start playing piano somewhere?" and he glared over at Sam Denoff as if to say, *Didn't I warn you this guy was a musician?*

Hal Moore's uneasiness was not unfounded, but it wasn't for a strictly music job that I left the radio station a few months later. Denoff and Persky were astounded and annoyed when I told them I was leaving. I was getting bored with the work. I jumped at the chance to go to work for RCA Victor Records at their East 24th Street headquarters. The new job, writing catalog copy and producing a monthly disc jockey newsletter, seemed to be closer to the heart of the music business, and besides, it paid $90 a week with medical benefits and retirement plan. In the face of all the temptations of the musical life, I clung to the conventional principles of my father and the rest of my family.

By this time I was living alone in a studio apartment on Greenwich Street, at the corner of 11th Street. I was seriously considering a life as a corporate executive. When I installed myself at RCA in a hangar-size room full of desks, I contemplated the glassed cubicles along the walls and imagined myself moving up into one of those, and who knew? Maybe even into one of the fancy private offices occupied by the bosses. Writing with phony enthusiasm about products and promotions came easily to me. I could write fast and effectively as long as the copy didn't have to be too literary. And wasn't the ad business a million laughs? My experience with Denoff and Persky at WNEW had showed me that the ad business was apparently populated by hip, funny guys who could make me laugh. I was seriously mistaken.

My main responsibility was to produce the monthly DJ newsletter, and it hadn't been refreshed in years. I churned out a couple of them during the first month, and everyone was very complimentary. My duties and responsibilities were easily and quickly accomplished, and I soon found myself with a lot of free time. The recording studios were in another part of the building, and understood to be off-limits to the office staff, so I couldn't sneak off to watch musicians the way I used to at the radio station. I decided to redesign the DJ newsletter, and I produced a dummy issue with a breezy new layout and a splashier way of displaying the new albums. I wrote a column about the changing music industry, and got a couple of Victor artists to contribute little blurbs about their new releases. I showed my souped-up version of the monthly pamphlet to my fellow workers. My boss, Ben Rosner, called me into his cubicle, and told me that my ideas were very interesting and the new promotion piece was very impressive, but I should just relax and do my job and stop trying to change things. "We have other people here who are responsible for making those decisions," he explained, "And would you blame them if they thought someone was crowding them or stepping on their toes?" I gulped as it hit me that he was talking about himself. "You do good work, Dave. But there's a time and a place for you to do your best work, and it's down the line a little bit." He was telling me to cool it because I was making him look bad. I was stunned by the concept of deliberately suppressing my best effort, and the corporation ethic of survival was revealed to me in a flash as Ben spoke from behind his desk. I blushed and said "Wow." Ben said, "You can go far here, but you have to be patient." I told him I understood, and I walked back to my desk in a daze. I leaned back in my swivel chair and began to think it over.

I had seen this kind of thinking in the air force, but I'd never for a moment considered that the air force would be my life. I thought that when I got plugged into the New York City media world, everyone would see how valuable I was, and it would only be a matter of doing my very best, and of course it would be a million laughs. I was wrong. There were not many laughs at RCA, and, more important, I discovered something about myself that could not be ignored. I didn't like having a boss. It was right around that time that I had a gig for a weekend playing Dixieland music in the Irish Catskills with some good players I had met at my friend Ed Bonoff's loft. I rode back to New York in trombonist Dick Rath's car. His girlfriend said, "You should have a job playing piano. You play too good to have a day job." Rath, who was driving, winced when he heard that. He was employed full-time as editor of *Yachting* magazine, and he and I had talked about his decision to keep a day job. We had agreed that the prudent and sensible thing to do was to make sure one had a reliable source of income, and then music could be on the side. That's what our dads had drilled into us. A bell rang inside me and I answered aloud, "You're right." Rath looked across at me and said, "Yes she is."

Debut at the Duplex

In April of 1958, I strolled over to Grove Street one night, stopped in at the Duplex, and had a drink in the basement bar, where the piano player was holding forth behind a midget piano—the sixty-six-key variety. I collared the tall, shambling piano player during intermission, and we had a long talk. His name was Billy Rubenstein, and he lived in the neighborhood too. He had heard me play in sessions in David X. Young's loft on Sixth Avenue. He was about to go on the road with

Kai Winding's four-trombone band, so the piano job at the Duplex was indeed up for grabs. "Hours are nine to two, six nights a week. Seventy-five dollars for the week. Would you be interested?" he asked. "Of course," I said. Billy arranged for me to get the gig, and I gave my two-week notice to RCA. Since the Duplex gig was to begin during the second week, I was anticipating five days of no sleep, but Ben Rosner told me after the first week that I needn't come back for week number two—they had already hired my replacement. I was walking on air as I left the building. A sense of relief swept over me as I realized I was finished being a junior executive. All I had to think about now was playing piano, and I could stay up all night if I felt like it. And that's exactly how I felt.

The Duplex gig was a killer. The hours were brutal. It was a very busy joint, crowded with maniacs of all imaginable genders. I played the sixty-six-key piano tucked under the staircase and there was barely room for me and the piano. If a bass player or horn player wanted to sit in (as happened once in a while), he would have to stand over near the bar.

They ran cabaret shows upstairs, featuring two or three acts that went on twice a night. A singer named Bea Barrett (I wonder what became of her) was "headlining" upstairs when I started working downstairs. One night during my first week I went upstairs to dig the show. Bea sang okay, but her pianist was terrible—no help at all. So I offered to play the show for her—I couldn't stand to hear the accompanist. After that, I spent every intermission upstairs playing the whole show—Bea Barrett plus the comic, who was the worst. I got no extra money for doing this. I kept it up for a couple weeks until the next singer was booked—Pat Suzuki from *Flower Drum Song*, who brought her own accompanist.

Tony, who owned the club, was an old-time tough guy in his seventies, and he was a hands-on manager who was always hanging around, glaring at me and checking his watch. Sometimes I had to wait until he closed up at 4 a.m. to get paid, and then he would tell me he didn't have it, and I'd have to come back the next day and ask for it. He chain-smoked cigars, and he would hawk up huge gobs of mucus and tobacco and spit them all over the floor, sometimes in the kitchen, sometimes in front of customers. Altogether, a splendid fellow.

During the day, I practiced on an upright I'd rented. The walls of my second-floor studio apartment on Greenwich Street were so thin that the piano was clearly audible all through the building. One day a distressed neighbor knocked at the door and begged me to stop. "I'm doing research and I work at home all day, and the piano playing is driving me crazy." I told him I was sorry, but I needed to practice and would continue to do so. I was cold about it, and it didn't bother me to take that attitude, whereas today I would be mortified if I thought I were bothering someone, and I would cease playing for a week. (Thirty years later, living alone in a Portland apartment, I bought an electric piano so I could play silently with headphones. I had my Kawai grand with me, but I didn't touch it for two years, because I didn't want anyone to overhear me.)

Thinking back on it, I don't blame my New York neighbor for being annoyed. I was working on my sight-reading, and it had to be a drag to hear me stumbling and fumbling around for hours at a time, playing at exaggerated slow tempos and making lots of mistakes. But I was getting better at it. Jeanne Bargy was the pianist at a restaurant a few doors up from the Duplex, and she would load me up with sheet music to take home. I would work on the stack for a few days and then trade it for another armload from Jeanne. I struggled through a couple of hundred pop-song sheets from Jeanne's library, and since I had started to rehearse with singers at my apartment, I was reading through lots of special arrangements and becoming familiar with the devices and maneuvers of the good songwriters. I could spot the quality stuff easily—Jerome Kern, Gershwin, Rodgers, Cole Porter, and especially Frank Loesser, who astonished me with his show songs.

I left after about three months. My chops were in good shape. I took a job for a week at Le Ruban Bleu, a swanky East Side boîte, where I wore a tux, played piano for three acts, and was the emcee. One of the acts was Stella Graham, a beautiful girl with a beautiful voice. We hit it off and began to keep steady company. By summer of 1958 I was spending a lot of time in Branford, Connecticut, where Stella was acting in a summer stock company. The company was housed dormitory style at the Montowese resort hotel, and I shared a room with an actor, Keith Charles, and Rick Sargent, who was set designer. I was musical director for the obligatory over-the-top old-fashioned melodrama called *Will the Mail Train Stop Tonight?*, and stayed onstage at the piano during the entire play, during which I pretended to get drunker and drunker and finally passed out in the finale.

At night everybody would gather around the piano in the hotel bar and sing with exuberant theatricality the show hits of the day. The material was all new to me, so I would spend the day woodshedding the sheet music. I discovered the songs from *Gypsy*, *Greenwillow*, and *Candide* and was knocked out by this literature, which wasn't exactly jazz-friendly or pop-song-oriented. Frank Loesser struck me as a major model for both words and music.

Kai Winding

Not long after that, everything changed when I took Bill Rubenstein's place as pianist with Kai Winding and went on the road.

I hurried by train back to New York from Connecticut when I heard that Kai Winding wanted me to audition at Nola Rehearsal Studio. His four-trombone band was going out on a tour and the piano chair was open, since Bill was leaving. Bill and I had met while he was playing at the Duplex, and he had arranged to get me hired there when he left to join Kai Winding. Now he was recommending me to succeed him as Kai's pianist. At Nola I met Ross Tompkins, who had just arrived in New York from Jacksonville, Florida, and was also auditioning for the piano chair. Winding ran through some of the charts and Ross and I alternated on piano. Ross was an ace reader, and my heart fell when I saw him sail through the piano parts. Hal Gaylor, the bass player, took me aside and said, "Kai is going to choose you because you're versatile, you can play any style." Kai and Gaylor and I went to Charlie's Tavern for dinner and Kai offered me the job. "Frish," he said, "you'll have to wear Bill Rubenstein's band jacket until the new one arrives. What size shall I order for you?" I told him, "Size 34." "Billy's jacket is a 46 long," Kai said. I told him, "That ought to cover it."

The first gig happened to be in New London, Connecticut. The whole gang from the Montowese Playhouse showed up to hear my debut with a big-name jazz group. Bill Rubenstein's mammoth coat was a hit. One of the trombone players, Tony Studd, switched jackets with me.

After the Connecticut job, the band set out from New York in two vehicles for a six-week tour of the southern states. We began with a two-week engagement at Trader Jon's in Pensacola, and then did one-nighters for four weeks, traveling through Florida, Georgia, Tennessee, the Carolinas, and Virginia, winding up at the Showboat in Washington, DC.

When we left New York for the southern tour, I loaded my luggage into the panel truck and climbed into Kai's white Chrysler station wagon, along with Kai and the trombone players George West, Johnny Messner, and Tony Studd. The panel truck, operated by bassist

Hal Gaylor and drummer Stu Martin, followed behind, loaded with instruments, music stands fronted with the band's name, and amplifiers, luggage and uniforms. And I mean loaded.

We drove south through a steady rainstorm. In Virginia, Kai turned to me in the backseat. "Frish, do you drive?" I told him I loved to drive, and he pulled to the side of the road and I took the wheel. Ten minutes later, I hit a patch of slimy road while making a big turn too fast, and before we knew what was happening, the Chrysler was off the road, half overturned in a gully full of mud. The five of us sat stunned in the tipped car, and nobody said a word until Kai broke the silence. "Nice going, Frish. Anybody hurt?" Everyone was okay, and when the panel truck pulled up behind us, Kai sent them to get a tow truck to pull us out of the muck. He never said another word to me about my reckless driving. "Could happen to anybody. Forget it." I was totally embarrassed and chagrined—my first day on the road with the band and I had piled up the Chrysler. The tow truck got us back on the highway, but I slunk back into the panel truck, and from then on through the end of the tour, I rode in the equipment truck with Hal and whoever the drummer turned out to be.

Up to that time I had been an occasional pot smoker and enjoyed it very much, but traveling in the truck with Hal and Stewie proved to be my introduction to full-time twenty-four-hour-a-day reefer madness. We had big laughs in the truck. Hal Gaylor was very talkative, as was I, and Stewie Martin was a great audience and an eager conversationalist. We talked about music and the people we knew in the business. The driving was exhausting, we got little rest, and we stayed alert and wired by popping green Dexamyl or orange Dexedrine tablets. The conversation was nonstop and intense and the laughs were gut-busting. Hal, who had practiced as an architect, gave long and detailed discourses on bricklaying, and had us entranced by the maneuvers and stratagems of placing headers and stretchers. I forgot what I talked about, but my truck mates would often chide me about my chattering on and on.

The two-week stay at Trader Jon's saloon was remarkable because we were billed opposite a one-man act who mimed and lip-synched to recorded music. It was raunchy and not very professional, and I couldn't figure out why Trader Jon's would book this kind of act when jazz was the featured attraction. It was even more mysterious when he suddenly added the great pianist Kenny Drew to the show as solo intermission act. The customers were drunk, crazed servicemen from the many nearby military bases, plus an unsavory collection of hookers, jazz fans, and assorted thugs and con artists. They couldn't care less about Kai Winding or Kenny Drew. "Kai who?"

One day I went to the beach, looked at the spectacular deep blue Gulf of Mexico, took off my shirt, sat down in the pure white sand, and began to read a book. I looked up and I was surrounded by a flock of sand crabs, transparent pink tubular creatures with black eyes on stalks. They were checking me out. When I got up to flee, they skittered away in all directions and disappeared into the sand. I walked quickly back to the motel and never returned to the beach.

After we left Florida, the trip was a blur of long road trips every day and sometimes at night. Marcy Lutes, a very good singer, had joined the band, and of course she sat in Kai's white Chrysler with the trombone players. The blue panel truck followed, with Stewie, Hal, and me howling with laughter over just about anything. Stu Martin left the band after the southern trip and went to Europe, where he became a modernist and somewhat of a free-jazz icon, playing mostly with black artists. Although Stu was Caucasian, fair-skinned with red hair, he chose to live as a black person, and I guess he pulled it off.

Kai's four-trombone band played slick, smooth arrangements, most of them by Kai himself. The current Columbia LP we were promoting was a collection of songs about states: "Indiana," "Tennessee Waltz," "Massachusetts," "Jersey Bounce," etc. My feature was "California, Here I Come," very fast, with four choruses of piano solo. As I remember, my chops were in great shape then. I'd only been a full-time musician for less than a year, but I had been playing practically every day and night since I strolled out of RCA Victor Corporation. I made a couple more trips with the Winding band, and then decided not to go back on the road. Stella and I were planning to get married, and I was pretty busy rehearsing singers in New York.

How History Almost Happened at the Page Three

Around the time I first came to New York, during the late '50s, I got a call from a piano player named Johnny Knapp. He asked if I would be interested in replacing him with the band at the Page Three. It was a two-piece band—piano and drums. "You have to play a continuous show," he told me. "The hours are 9 p.m. to 4 a.m., and the pay is seventy-five a week." I told him I would be interested.

The Page Three was a cabaret on Seventh Avenue a block south of the Village Vanguard. I was living right across the street on Waverly Place, and could dash out of my apartment five minutes before we hit, and even dash back and forth during intermissions. I took the gig.

I thought I was hip, but I wasn't ready for the Page Three. When I first walked in, it took me a while to realize that most of the staff and many of the customers were dressed as the opposite sex. It was like a museum of sexual lifestyles. I knew nothing of this.

The musical part was equally intimidating. The policy was continuous entertainment, and although we must have been provided with intermissions, my memory is that the drummer and I were never off the stage. Six entertainers did three shows a night. They rotated out of a stable of ten so that each entertainer worked four or five nights a week. This was a hell of a lot of music and paper to deal with, since everybody needed rehearsals, and some of the performers came with thick books of arrangements.

Kiki Hall was the emcee. After the first rehearsal I had to take Kiki's music home and work on it. He did risqué patter and naughty lyrics, and there was a lot of ad lib accompaniment and stops and starts, and it all went by very fast. Kiki did Noël Coward material like "Mad Dogs and Englishmen" and "Don't Put Your Daughter on the Stage, Mrs. Worthington," and some Dwight Fiske material, and other stuff I had never heard of. He was ruthless about the piano part, tolerated no mistakes, and demanded extra rehearsals during the week. He was a pain in the ass.

The hostess, Jackie Howe, was a solidly built woman with a big friendly smile who always dressed in a tweed business suit. She liked jazz musicians, and she sang obscure songs like "Mississippi Dreamboat" and "Like a Ship in the Night." I was learning a lot of unfamiliar and interesting material.

The rest of the cast was a jumble of characters, talented and untalented: There was Kerri April, who dressed in a tuxedo and made up his face to look like a woman, and Laurel Watson, who was a terrific rhythm and blues singer, and Bubbles Kent, a female bodybuilder who did a strip dance to "Top Hat, White Tie, and Tails." Tiny Tim, who was just beginning to do his act, was from time to time a member of the cast, although during the months I worked there he appeared only a couple of nights, subbing for one of the other acts. I remember the occasions chiefly because of the fact that Jimmy Olin and I were able to get off the stage for a cigarette or two while Tiny accompanied himself on the ukulele or whatever it was. Jimmy and I would listen from the front bar, and we had some good laughs, but the fact was that in the context of the Page Three staff, entertainers, and clientele, Tiny Tim didn't seem all that bizarre.

The Unique Monique was especially unrewarding to play for. She was a beautiful blond Viking who was apparently buffaloed by the prospect of singing a song, and seemed to have borrowed someone else's hands and feet for the ordeal. She sang "Guess Who I Saw Today," and at the end she would jab a finger toward some poor guy sitting at a front table and give him the "I saw YOOOOO" on the major seventh, dismally out of tune.

What Jimmy and I looked forward to each night was Sheila Jordan. Sheila was magic. The customers would stop gabbing and all the entertainers would turn their attention to Sheila and the whole place would be under her spell. She was doing "If You Could See Me Now" and "Baltimore Oriole" and some of the other material that she subsequently put on record.

During my time at the Page Three I began to grasp the fundamentals of how to be a helpful accompanist, and by the time I was ready to move on even Kiki Hall was pleased and confident with the way I played for him. In fact, when I told him I was leaving (to join Sol Yaged at the Metropole), Kiki threw a tantrum. "Oh no! Who's going to play my Noël Coward material?" "I got just the guy," I told him.

About a week earlier I had met the pianist Herbie Nichols, who was a unique jazz stylist, very advanced and adventurous, and as unorthodox and original as Thelonious Monk. But I'd heard Nichols play in a conventional situation, and I immediately understood that this guy could be musical and appropriate in all kinds of contexts. I sounded him about the Page Three. He was interested.

Sure enough, Herbie was a hit with the cast, and became the new pianist. I stopped in one night to dig him, and Jackie Howe gave me the big smile and the "okay" sign. Herbie sounded like a million bucks and everybody was happy.

A few weeks later I dropped by the Page Three after my gig. When Kiki Hall saw me, he began hissing "It's your fault!" and Jackie Howe had to restrain him from going for my throat. The Unique Monique was onstage, and she seemed even more lost than usual. "I saw YOOO," she sang on that dismal major seventh, and the pianist resolved the chord a half step down so Monique's note became the tonic. It was shocking and unearthly, and the customers began to laugh. Monique stumbled off the stage in tears. I looked at the pianist and I didn't recognize him. Herbie Nichols had sent a sub. The other singers were sitting in a booth, all very upset, and they were refusing to go on. Kiki was climbing the walls, and Bubbles Kent had gone home. Sheila Jordan greeted me with a big smile. "You really missed something tonight," she said. "You should have heard Kiki's show. You should have heard 'Mad Dogs and Englishmen.' It was really out there! You know who that is on piano, don't you? You don't? That's Cecil Taylor," she told me. "Herbie sent him to sub. He's been here all night, played for everyone. You've never heard a show like this in your life."

I thought that over for a moment, wishing I had it on tape. Then a thought hit me. "Sheila," I said. "Dare I ask? Could it be true? Did Tiny Tim perform tonight?" "No, damn it," she said. "Wouldn't that have been priceless?"

"Well, Tiny Tim doesn't use piano anyway," I said, "so it wouldn't have happened."

Sheila said, "Oh yes, it would have happened. Cecil would have played. Cecil would have insisted on playing."

Herbie Nichols came back the next night and I assume all was forgiven. Herbie died not long after this took place. My path and Sheila's path still cross once in a while, and naturally I go into my Page Three routines. I can still get a laugh with my Monique imitation, but the Page Three survivors list is dwindling, and there are few of us left to share the memories, real and imagined. But I keep the stories going, and I have been known in weak moments to announce that I once saw Cecil Taylor play for Tiny Tim. So let the word go forth now that it never happened. I only wish it had happened. Of course, I'm assuming that they never got together privately.

How to Impress Your Parents in New York

In the summer of 1958 my parents came to New York for a few days to visit me. We were strolling in the Village one afternoon. I pointed to a young fellow who was walking near us. "I know that guy," I said. "He plays trumpet, and I met him at a jam session the other night." I stepped over and said hello to the guy. I introduced him to my mom and dad, and we chatted on Sixth Avenue and Eighth Street. He seemed a little uneasy and upset, and he told us that he and his friends were being questioned by the police regarding an attempt to blow up the Statue of Liberty the week before. Then he apologized for rushing off, said goodbye, and walked away. My mother was politely concerned. My dad was not thrilled to say the least; he remained pretty glum the rest of the day, and he didn't seem interested in meeting any more of my friends. "So he tried to blow it up?" he said. My mom corrected him, "Suspected of trying to blow it up." I never ran into that guy again. He seemed friendly enough, but I didn't enjoy his playing.

The Union Floor

The offices of Musicians' Local 802 occupied the upper floors of Roseland Ballroom, on 52nd Street west of Broadway. Hundreds of jobbing musicians gathered every Wednesday afternoon on the main floor—the union floor, as it was commonly called—the vast Roseland dance floor. From the stage, a union guy intoned names on the public address, and that's what you'd hear as you entered the lobby of Roseland: "Paul Gaglio, Paul Gaglio, Paul Gaglio . . . Chizzick Epstein, Chizzick Epstein, Chizzick Epstein . . . Shorty Allen, Shorty Allen, Shorty Allen . . . Bobby Donovan, Bobby Donovan, Bobby Donovan . . ." The contractors and the sidemen were gathered in groups scattered around the dance floor. Entering through the lobby you would pass the junkies, usually engaged in confidential conversations, and often hitting you up for fifty cents. If you walked up one floor, there were the recording musicians waiting in line to collect paychecks at the windows. Downstairs on the floor, you would find the Latin musicians along the first-base line. The road musicians and dance bands were along the third base line; the jazz musicians tended to cluster between home plate and the pitcher's mound. The big-time club date contractors would gather around center field near the stage, and there was always a crowd buzzing around them, because for jobbing freelance musicians those were the best-paying gigs. There was no reason for me to venture into right field, the Greek and Middle Eastern section.

I could always find somebody I knew on the union floor, and get involved in some kind of action—gig, a weekend, a rehearsal, a jam session, a summer job, some smoke. My friend the drummer Maurice Mark would holler, "Davie! Davie! Follow me. Irving Grauer is looking for a piano player. Irving! Irving! Here's Davie Frishberg, the piano player I was telling you about." Grauer carried a clipboard around with him and wanted to know, "Does he know the tunes?" (I was always tempted to answer, "All but one," but who knew if these people had a sense of humor?) Often, the plum jobs were reserved for those players who were loyal and could do the contractor a favor. "Look, if you'll cover the next three Friday-Saturdays for me in Long

Island, I got a private party on West End Avenue that pays very well." So you had to schlep out to Long Beach and back six times to get the one good gig. Sometimes I said okay. Seven gigs, cash off the books, it's hard to pass up. But you never knew; saying yes might get you in a mess.

The Accordion Episode

In 1958, when I was single and just beginning to freelance, I got a call from Johnny Knapp, a busy pianist that I knew. "I can't make Saturday's gig with Sid Zeiler. Can you do it for me? Zeiler's a big club date contractor in Long Island, and if he likes you, there's a ton of work there; it would be a great connection for you. Pays seventy-five dollars."

I said, "Yeah, sure. Where is it?"

"It's out in Long Beach, a big banquet from seven to eleven. You play accordion?"

I said. "No, I certainly don't."

"Well, you're gonna need to bring an accordion. I'll give you directions to my house. You can borrow one of my accordions and use it on the gig. I'll show you how to play it. You'll catch on right away. You got a car? You'll need a car for the accordion."

"I can borrow a car."

"Great. And wear a tux."

I borrowed John Beal's Saab on Saturday afternoon and drove out to Johnny Knapp's house in south Queens. "Here's the accordion you're gonna play. Sit down. Here, you put arms through here and here— that's right. No, don't touch the buttons, forget your left hand, you're just gonna use your right hand. It's just a keyboard. Sit down, play some notes, that's right. Play some chords. See? And just use your left arm to pump very gently, don't touch the buttons. Right! You sound great, man. You'll be fine. Sid Zeiler's gonna love you. Bring the accordion back to my house; I'll be home by that time. Here's how you pack it up. I'll carry it out to the car for you."

I drove to the gig and wrestled the accordion out of the Saab. It was heavy. With the case, it probably weighed fifty pounds. I could barely manage to drag the monster to the banquet room. I unpacked the instrument and placed it at the piano near my left ankle. Sid Zeiler seemed cordial, the band was easy to play with, and everything was going well. After the first set, Zeiler came over to me and said, "Okay, they're eating. You'll stroll now with bass and saxophone."

"Stroll?"

"Yeah, you walk around the tables and play while they eat. Pick up the accordion. You never done this?"

"Oh sure," I said, struggling with the clasp that kept the bellows folded. The accordion fell open with a heavy sigh, and I grabbed the arm straps and lifted the accordion to my hips while I attempted to stand upright, which I had never tried to do before; I had only played it while I was seated with the instrument in my lap.

The bass player said, "You ready? Let's go. 'Tenderly' in E-flat." The sax player played the three pickup notes while I groped for the keyboard with my right hand to find the E-flat major seventh chord. To my horror, the keyboard was now slanted toward the floor and hidden from view behind the heaving bellows. The instrument was too heavy for me to hold on to, and I clutched desperately to keep the accordion from hitting the floor. My left arm was pressed against three rows of buttons and the accordion was roaring like a hundred voices screaming for help. My right hand was forming a cluster of wrong notes, and all this was fortissimo to say the least, and "Tenderly" was now well into measure number three. The accordion was blasting out terrible coughs and gasps. I was staggering around the empty dance floor trying to hold on to the accordion without touching the buttons or the keyboard. The sax player and the bassist stopped playing and gaped as I nearly fell into a table where six people with shrimp cocktails drew back in horror. "Excuse me," I said. "This isn't my instrument." I limped back to the piano and disengaged the straps from my shoulders. Sid Zeiler was there. "Put that away, and don't touch it again," he said.

I returned the accordion to Johnny Knapp's house on my way home. I told him, "You didn't tell me I'd have to stand up and walk around. You can't see the keys that way." "Sorry," Johnny said. "I forgot to mention that. Strolling's another story."

I never heard from Sid Zeiler. I don't suppose Knapp did either. It's hard to believe that I got myself into that kind of situation, but when you need the gig, I guess you instinctively answer yes. I did learn that if they ask you to double on accordion, the prudent response would be, "Seated only."

190 Waverly Place

Before I finally left New York to take a television job on the West Coast, I was living very frugally and had grown accustomed to shopping and spending carefully. Stella and I lived for over eleven years in a one-bedroom apartment at 190 Waverly Place with a tiny cramped kitchen where only one person at a time could work. Our rent was $90 in 1960, and had risen to $115 when I left in 1971.

I owned three cars during my stay in the city. The one I bought from Bill Takas was the most remarkable. Takas was an excellent bass player who worked alongside me on many and varied occasions, and I often hung out listening to records in his Bleecker Street pad, where he introduced me to the choicest contemporary music: Ray Charles, Otis Redding, Burt Bacharach and Dionne Warwick, the Beach Boys. Takas, who raced Porsches, owned several cars and kept a battered

1955 Volkswagen convertible to drive around in town. The rear end was crushed to within an inch of the engine. The two of us stood on the curb one day eyeing the old jalopy when Takas said, "I'll sell it to you for seventy-five bucks." "That sounds great," I said, "but what about that rear end? It's practically in the backseat." Takas said, "Wait here. I'll be right back." He came back with a chain, hitched it to a fire hydrant, and connected it to the rear end of the yellow Volks. Then he inched the car forward until the rear end was pulled out to near factory specification. I drove the car for five years after that, parking it on the street each night. One morning I found Takas's note on my windshield: WANT TO SELL YOUR CAR? I called him and told him I wouldn't take less than seventy-five for it. He paid me, drove the car away, and I never saw it again. One day I recognized the radio in Takas's Porsche. "Is that my Blaupunkt?" I asked. Takas replied, "Why do you think I wanted the car back?"

My first visit to Takas's apartment on Bleecker and Christopher took place in 1958, when I had just moved into the Village and Joel Upin and I were sharing an apartment on West Fourth Street. I climbed up four flights to Takas's place one night after a gig. It was one small room with a kitchenette, and it contained everything in Bill's life except his automobiles. One of the main conversation pieces was the Porsche engine placed on newspapers in the middle of the floor. Bill explained that he worked on it from time to time. I made occasional visits to the Bleecker Street pad during the ensuing thirty-five years, and the Porsche engine was always there, still in the middle of the floor.

Subsequently, I owned a bright blue 1960 Volkswagen with psychedelic daisies painted on it. I never bothered to remove them. It didn't seem important. The life of a parked car on the streets of New York was perilous, and it was pointless to dress up your car or maintain it cosmetically, because it would only become a more tempting target for theft or vandalism. I paid $300 for it, and when it was stolen after a couple of years I didn't mind. I was saved the trouble of disposing of it. I bought a blue 1962 Toyota Corona for $750, and drove it for several years until I left New York in spring of 1971.

Stella and I lived on the top floor rear of a five-story building. Our living room window opened onto the rear fire escape, so 5F was an easy mark for burglars. We got hit five times during my eleven-plus-year residence there. They always grabbed small stuff like radios or hi-fi equipment, stuff they could carry away quickly and easily and get some cash for. All of the burglaries were daytime occurrences while we were absent. We installed heavy folding locked gates on the windows, and a "police lock" pole on the entrance door. The last intrusion was very upsetting. Around noon I came home from a short trip to the bank, opened the door, and saw directly before me a man, head down, climbing through our living room window. I grabbed the police lock pole and confronted him when he looked up and saw me. Like a flash he backed out the window and was gone up the fire escape in an instant. After that, I would see the guy in the neighborhood. Once I ran into him at the newsstand on Sheridan Square. We nodded to each other. "How ya doin'?" he murmured.

In later years, browsing in books and articles about folk music, I saw references to my apartment building, 190 Waverly Place, the scene of late-night folk sessions with Bob Dylan, Pat Sky, Dave Van Ronk, Carolyn Hester, and other pioneers of the musical revolution. I remember coming home from the Metropole or the Half Note in the wee hours, feeling no pain and hollering down the airshaft at the hootenanny raging down on the third floor. "That's shit you're playing! You know that, don't you?" I knew that Van Ronk lived in the building, and some other people involved in the folk scene, but I had no idea that these people were prominent and influential performers. To me it was just amateurs playing and singing. Leadbelly at three o'clock in the morning? Gimme a break, folks. Even the Midnight Special stops.

Re: Bob Dylan

(To Neal McCabe re: a previous conversation)

We all knew people like Bob Dylan. We met them in college. Vaguely talented guys who could strum guitars and sing angry songs about the Spanish Civil War. The girls went for it. But these guys didn't have illusions about professional music as a vocation. Most of them stowed the guitars after graduation. The concept of the rock star hadn't been invented yet. I wonder if, if he hadn't been discovered and distracted by Albert Grossman and the other thieves and flatterers, Dylan might have wound up back in St. Paul teaching creative writing at Macalester College.

Anyway, seems to me "Blowin' in the Wind" doesn't make any sense. I don't get it. The lyric asks rhetorical questions and then dismisses them with a vaguely patronizing conclusion that doesn't address the questions at all. The message of the song seems to be, "You're full of shit, so don't ask," which is neither profound nor helpful. But isn't that a recurring underlying message in other Dylan songs? Hey let's face it, that's why Dylan never made it.

For my money, Hal David and Alan and Marilyn Bergman are the best lyricists of the Dylan years. And for artful thoughtful lyric writing that's both magic and meaningful, I'll take Hal David's "Alfie," and various lyrics by Paul Williams, Carolyn Leigh, Fran Landesman, and Bob Dorough. Among the younger writers of today I respond to Lorraine Feather, who's smart and crafty as hell.

Thanks for listening,

D. Frishberg

Re: Dorough

I knew about Bob Dorough since 1956, when I spotted his LP in a record store in Salt Lake City and listened to it with headphones in the sampling booth. "I gotta meet this guy," I said to myself, and bought the record. When I got to New York a year later I had his phone number, but I learned that he had recently moved to Los Angeles. It was in the early 1960s, when Bob had returned to New York, that Blossom Dearie introduced me to him.

I was just beginning to write songs then. Bob came to my apartment one day and we played our songs for each other. I was dazzled. The two of us got together a couple times after that and attempted to write songs at the piano, but we both were shy about suggesting things, and we didn't make any progress.

I told him, "Let's try this: I'll write a lyric and bring it to you, and you set it to music." Bob agreed, and the result was "I'm Hip." It was my first collaboration with another songwriter, and thereafter I have never attempted to work that way—with my lyric first. Instead, I sometimes supply words to a melody written by another composer.

The Sixth Avenue Loft

I was doing a lot of jamming myself during those days and nights. I would go to W. Eugene Smith's loft on Sixth Avenue. Smith, the famous photographer, was never around. At least, I never saw him on the premises. There was music going on around the clock, and I learned years later that W. Eugene Smith was recording everything from upstairs, hanging a microphone from a hole in the floor.

That's where I first met and heard, among others, Dave McKenna; Bill Takas; Ronnie Free, the great drummer from South Carolina; bassist John Beal, guitarist Sam Brown; and the legendary tenor sax player Fred Greenwell from Seattle. Freddy was a freakishly talented jazz player who played entirely by ear and couldn't discuss music in terms of notes or chords, sharps or flats. He loved to play and would play all night and into the next morning, going without sleep for days until the Dexedrine was gone. Then you wouldn't see him for a week or so, but he'd be back at the loft after that.

Drugs were a big part of the scene at the Sixth Avenue loft and the other lofts in Lower Manhattan. The needle guys would tend to their business privately in the bathroom, and I was never tempted to join in on that side of the fence. The idea of injecting myself made me queasy, and I didn't want to know about it, but I didn't care if my colleagues chose that road; that way of life was not at all uncommon in the jazz culture among players and listeners alike. I participated in the pot-smoking and eagerly dabbled in Dexedrine, Dexamyl, and other amphetamine pills. I loved the feeling I got when I took the uppers, but the inevitable despondency that followed was so fierce that after a couple years of that vicious seesaw I decided to use those substances sparingly, and finally not at all.

Igor and Pat

During the summer of 1959 in New York a lashing rainstorm began suddenly while I was walking on the East Side. I ducked into the nearest doorway, which happened to be a side entrance to the FAO Schwarz toy emporium. There I huddled with two other men who were taking refuge. I glanced at the short elderly man next to me and my heart began to pound—Igor Stravinsky. Next to Igor was a tall, younger man whom I subsequently identified from a photograph. It was Robert Craft, Stravinsky's collaborator and biographer. I was staring at Stravinsky, surprised to see how small he was, and trying to think of something to say that would be apt. I thought of mentioning *The Firebird*, or maybe whistling a snatch of *Petrouchka*. The two men stared straight ahead and seemed annoyed that they were held up by the rain. Finally I spoke up and said, "Excuse me." Stravinsky and Craft turned to me, but I found myself unable to speak. I didn't want to sink into mere gushing, and I became embarrassed. "I'd better go inside," I said, and briskly entered the store. There I stumbled and nearly ran into a customer who was engaged in animated conversation with a salesperson across the counter. I recognized him at once. It was Pat Boone. "I beg your pardon," I said, and continued on into the stuffed-animal department, where I was able to collect my thoughts. "You gotta be on your toes in this burg." I told myself.

Ava and Me

During the summer of 1961, when I was with Kenny Davern's band at Nick's Tavern in the Village, drummer Cliff Leeman, bassist Jack Six, and I would often spend intermissions at Hymie's Bar on Sheridan Square, where the drinks were fifty cents instead of $2 (Nick's price). One night there was one other customer sitting alone at the bar, and we realized that it was indeed Ava Gardner. I raised my glass and called to her, "We'd like to buy you a taste." She said, "I would be delighted." We all clinked glasses, and she explained why she was alone in Hymie's Bar. "My friend the matador is in that joint," she said, indicating the Spanish nightclub across the street, "and he's about to get the shit kicked out of him. I told him when he's finished screwing around over there, he'd find me over here." I was in love with her for a moment, but by the time we were back on the bandstand at Nick's I had forgotten all about her. We haven't spoken since.

Bud Freeman

In the autumn of 1960 I was playing at Eddie Condon's on East 56th Street with Bud Freeman, and early one afternoon I was practicing in my fifth-floor apartment in Greenwich Village when the doorbell rang and I heard Bud Freeman's voice on the speaker. "Dave, my wife and I are strolling in the neighborhood, and I knew you lived here. I wonder if we might come up for a visit?" I was startled and said, "Why sure! C'mon up, we're in 5F." I hung up and Stella said, "Bud Freeman?" I said, "Bud Freeman. I hardly know the guy except on the bandstand. I don't get it."

The Freemans arrived at the door. Bud was sharp in a tweed sport coat with a tie. The women were introduced with much genial chatter, and the four of us sat down in the small living room. Hospitalities were in order, and an hour later we had exhausted our modest inventory of scotch and vodka. "We're on our way anyway," Bud said. "We're just going to stroll around a bit and then take a cab home. See you at Condon's. Cheers!" It was about ten minutes later that Stella and I remembered that all the bars were closed until sundown because it was Election Day.

A self-proclaimed frustrated actor, Bud was onstage pretty much all the time, and the role he seemed to be auditioning for was the leading man in a play by Noël Coward or P. G. Wodehouse. He didn't affect an English accent, but his carriage and delivery were definitely upper class, as was his wardrobe. In a taped interview, saxophonist Lester Young, who enjoyed Bud's playing, responded to a mention of Bud Freeman by crooning the words *Ivy Dyvie*.

Bud would step to the microphone and tug his cuff links before he began to play. He was a hard swinger with a big sound and an odd assembly of dazzling maneuvers, and while he influenced a lot of tenor saxophonists, he was not easy to imitate, and nobody ever sounded like him. (Except maybe Sam Margolis of Boston, who took pains to sound like Bud and came close.)

Bud was impressed by class and breeding. He asked me to recommend a bass player, so I mentioned Steve Swallow, whom I had recently met at a loft session. When I told him that Steve was young—only seventeen or eighteen—and Bud said, "He's too young. He won't know any songs, he lacks the experience, he's not seasoned enough, and I've never heard him play." I replied that Steve knew plenty of old tunes because he had played with a Dixieland band at Yale. Bud's face lit up. "A Yale man! Will you call him for me, Dave?"

In February 1961 we did two weeks at the Theatrical Lounge in Cleveland, with Mickey Sheen on drums, and the eighteen-year-old Steve Swallow. We drove in Mickey Sheen's station wagon, leaving New York on a bitter cold morning. We loaded in the drums, the bass, and the luggage, and Steve and I headed for the backseat, but Bud would have none of it. "No, I'll take the backseat. I'll be perfectly comfortable sitting in the rear, it's no problem. No, I insist! Don't you see, I'm the one who won't be driving. You'll all be taking shifts helping with the driving, so it's perfectly fair and reasonable that I should take a backseat, so to speak." So Bud climbed in the backseat with the neck of the bass between him and Swallow, and we were off to Cleveland.

Ten minutes later we crossed the George Washington Bridge into New Jersey. Bud said, "Mickey, you are going to turn the heater on, aren't you?" Mickey said, "The heater's on, Bud. You want a little more heat? I'll turn it up." Bud said, "Yes, please do! I'm about to freeze back here."

A few minutes later Bud said, "Is there a blanket or something I could put over my feet?" Mickey cranked the heater up a little more. We drove a few miles and Bud said quietly, "Steve, aren't you freezing? I can't see your face, because of this damn bass fiddle between us. It's getting a little claustrophobic back here, wouldn't you agree?"

Mickey said, "Bud, I'll stop at the next turnoff and you and Frishberg can change places."

So we pulled off the big switch in a gas station in Parsippany. Bud was all smiles when he snuggled into the front passenger seat and said "Ah, this is much better. Why didn't we think of this in the first place?" We drove straight through to Cleveland, and Bud was good company during the rest of the journey.

We stayed in the Hollenden Hotel. Freeman, Steve Swallow, and I sometimes had breakfast or lunch together in the hotel coffee shop. Bud loved Steve's bass playing, and he was indeed tickled by the fact that Steve had attended Yale. He would drop Shakespearian references and make other remarks about the theater and literature, as if he expected some kind of Yale-inspired response from Steve. He woke me one morning with a phone call from the lobby: "Steve and I are in the coffee shop if you'd like to join us. We're going to talk about *Hamlet*."

One afternoon, Steve invited me and Bud to his hotel room to listen to tapes. He was eager for Bud to hear John Coltrane and Ornette Coleman. Bud listened patiently to Coltrane's "Naima" and made polite comments. When he heard Ornette he burst out laughing. "That's not new!" He said. "We used to play that way when we were kids, just to be funny! He's serious, isn't he? Or is he making fun of music like we used to do in Chicago? Sometimes we'd play like that and the people weren't laughing, and they would applaud and think we were brilliant!" Swallow was a little downcast, while Bud guffawed over the new music. Steve brought a couple of Monk tunes to rehearsal and Bud played them and sounded oddly at home with the idiom. I don't think we played them on the gig, though.

The Rogers drum company engaged a Cleveland photographer to make formal shots of the four of us posing with Mickey Sheen's Rogers drum set. The caption was puzzling: "BUD FREEMAN Featuring MICKEY SHEEN and the QUARTET."

A few months later Freeman was planning a recording date with bassist Bob Haggart, drummer Don Lamond, and myself. Bud and I rehearsed the material at Condon's for three afternoons, and Bud was very careful about his selection of tunes, and very exacting in devising little riffs and figures that we rehearsed over and over, just the two of us. We chose about a dozen titles and worked up simple routines.

We recorded one afternoon at a studio on the mezzanine floor of the Great Northern Hotel on 57th Street. I was introduced to Haggart and Lamond, and Bud paced with his saxophone, warming up with furious arpeggios. Then he said, "Gentlemen, we have three hours, and we have a lot of material to record, so let's not waste any time. Does everyone know 'You're a Sweetheart'?" This was not on the list we had prepared. "Not me," I said. Haggart quickly showed me the changes, and we were off. The song ended and Bud said, "Let's go to the next one. How about 'Paper Moon'? Everyone knows that." We three sidemen shrugged and began to play 'Paper Moon.' When it was over, Bud quickly suggested another song out of left field, and then another, nothing from the list. I laid the list aside and forgot about it. We winged the whole date and finished in three hours with fourteen tunes, nearly all of them first takes. We didn't use any of the songs Bud and I had prepared.

Neither Haggart nor I was familiar with Harold Arlen's "Last Night When We Were Young," so Freeman provided a sheet music copy for us to read. The song was pretty mysterious, particularly in the bridge with the melody weaving around on non-chord tones. Haggart stood behind me and read the piano music over my shoulder. By the time we finished reading through it, I was beginning to grasp the harmony and the structure. Then Bud decided he wanted to play it a tone down, and I gulped and agreed. I swear I heard Haggart gulp too. So I penciled in the changes and we made a take in the new key. Bud called to the control room, "Did you record that? I hope so."

I prevailed on Bud to let us make one more take, because we were starting to learn the song and how it should be played. He grumbled, but granted us a second crack at it. Haggart was relieved too, and we congratulated ourselves on an enlightened second take. Freeman kept glancing at the clock.

Bud gave me a hug at the end of the date, and said cheerfully, "You know, Dave, when it's your date, then it's okay to ask for another take." I told Bud I understood, but that since this is the first time my name would appear on liner notes, I wanted to make sure I didn't come off too clumsy. I didn't mention the three days of earnest preparation, and neither did Bud.

The LP came out on an English label, and years later I found a copy at Ray Avery's record store in Burbank. I took it home and listened to myself and Haggart tightrope-walking through the Harold Arlen sheet music, and I felt the same uneasiness I had felt in the studio. I got to know Bob Haggart better in later years, and we laughed about the famous Bud Freeman date. Haggart said it could have been the world's record for number of songs ground out in a three-hour session.

When Bud visited L.A. in 1982 we played together one afternoon at my house. He said, "Remember that thing we worked out on 'Three Little Words'?" and he began to run through the routines that we had rehearsed for the record date twenty years before. He actually remembered everything, every detail. Go figure.

He was a wonderful jazz player with a hot style all his own, and had a rare talent: He could join a three-horn ensemble and instantly fake a perfect fourth part. He generated hot rhythm. I enjoyed playing with him very much.

Judy and Me

I only recently learned of Johnny Mercer's longtime love affair with

Judy Garland. Wow, what a story that must be. In New York in the mid-'60s I was playing with Anita O'Day at the Half Note, and one night in walks Charlie Cochran, Anita's crony, and with him is this frail shadowy figure that I realize is Judy Garland, for Chrissake. Naturally, Anita invites her up on the stage, there is a mild protestation from Judy, and now she stands at the microphone, and the customers are going berserk.

"What shall I sing? I don't know what to sing!" Judy is saying, and I realize that she is speaking to me. Like the piano player always knows the answer. But I was off the hook because people in the audience were hollering, "'Ova the Rainbow'! 'Ova the Rainbow'!" She turned to me and said, "Let's do that," and waited for me to give her the introduction or the note or something. I asked her, "What key?" And she stares at me with a haunted look and says, "I have no idea."

Anita comes to the rescue and shouts at me, "What's the original?" I yell back, "E-flat." So Anita yells, "Then her key is a fourth away from that! That's the way it works for females! They're always a fourth away from the original key!" This is absurd, of course, but I give Judy her notes in B-flat, and she says no, that's too high. John Poole, Anita's drummer, shouts, "They wrote the song for her! They wrote it in her key!" This makes sense, so I cue Judy in E-flat and she begins to sing. When she finishes, people are stamping and shouting, and Judy says, "Hey this is great! Let's do another one," and looks to me for direction. So now Anita takes over and says to Judy, "Just sing along with me," and the two of them do a couple of standards. They tear the place up, and Judy leaves the stage and joins Charlie Cochran at a table in the back. When the set was over, it was closing time and I was preparing to leave. Charlie Cochran told me that Judy wanted to speak to me, and he took me to the table and left Miss Garland and me alone to have a conversation.

She leaned across the table and spoke in an intimate tone. "Did you see how nervous I was? Did you hear my knees knocking?" Then she spent about five minutes telling me how frightened she was to perform in front of people, and how she had suffered from chronic stage fright and ravaging insecurity since she was five years old. "Have some more wine," she said, and then launched into semicoherent babbling about her approaching trip to England. "This is my idea," she began as if she had just thought of it. "I want you to come with me to England, and I want you to play for me there. I want you to get a show together for me, and I want you to be my musical director."

I squirmed and mumbled something about having to think it over, and she became disappointed and sad. Her face turned grim. "I thought we'd be great together," she said. I was a little stunned by all this and very uncomfortable, because she wasn't making much sense. Charlie came back to the table about that time, thank God, and that was the end of the famous conversation with Judy Garland.

Subsequently, in L.A., when I wrote songs for the *Funny Side* TV series, the musical director was Jack Elliott, who had spent years as Garland's pianist and conductor. When I told him of my conversation at the Half Note, he rolled his eyes, flapped his wrist, and remained discreetly quiet.

About fifteen years later I read Mel Tormé's book about working with Judy Garland on her TV show, and he tells of how Judy would "discover" a new piano player and enlist him as her personal accompanist and musical director, and then proceed to drive him up the wall with her shifting whims, her neurotic neediness, and her unpredictable predilection for romantic episodes. I think Mercer must have had himself quite a handful.

~

For a while in 1961–'62 I was pianist-conductor with Dick Haymes and Fran Jeffries, an ultimately unpleasant job that ended with him owing me money—which I never got, by the way. We played two weeks at the Beverly Hills in Newport, Kentucky, right outside of Cincinnati, (during the World Series with the Reds vs. Yankees with Yogi Berra, Mickey Mantle, Roger Maris, et al.) We traveled with lead trumpet (George Triffon), lead alto (Bobby Donovan), bass (Bucky Calabrese), and drums (Steve Little). Local musicians filled the rest of the chairs to make seven brass and five reeds. I rehearsed the band the day before, and thereafter gave downbeats and cutoffs from the piano. The Cincinnati musicians were first-rate.

On the last night, everybody was packing up and saying so long and shaking hands. I said goodbye to a couple of trombone players, one of whom asked me to give his regards to several musicians we all knew. "Tell them Bill Rank says hello."

"You're Bill Rank?"

"Yeah."

"From Jean Goldkette's band?" I swear I said that.

"That's right. Well, got to be going. Nice meeting you all, bye."

And he disappeared into the Kentucky night. I'd been calling him Bill for two weeks and now I find out he's Bill Rank! Bill Rank, star trombonist of the New York studio scene during the 1920s and '30s, colleague of Bix Beiderbecke, Hoagy Carmichael, Frankie Trumbauer, Eddie Lang, Adrian Rollini, Paul Whiteman! And all this time, I could have hung with him backstage. What stories he could have told me. Once again, you gotta be on your toes, you gotta pay attention.

Anita O'Day

I'm not a fan of Anita O'Day, having played quite a few gigs with her in New York and L.A. Even made an album in L.A. with just piano and her. Thank God it was never released, because I played like a pig. For me, she was a total drag to play music with. Her tortured phrasing and abominable scatting were terrible turnoffs, and she went out of her way to be difficult and unpredictable, and always in front of an audience so that she could chide the musicians and get laughs. When she sang ad lib out of tempo with just piano or guitar she would insert extra words and trip up the accompanist. I knew several musicians who refused to play for her. Twenty-five years later in New York one musician walked off the bandstand at the Half Note when she was asked to sit in. I witnessed it; I was playing piano.

The only time in my life I ever left the piano in the middle of a song was with her, at the Riverboat Room in the Empire State Building. She was singing with piano "On a Clear Day" out of tempo, and it was so horrible that I got up from the piano and walked right off the stage and out the door. Maurice Mark, the drummer, ran after me and grabbed me by the arm. "I don't blame you, Davey," he said, and then he ran back to his drums. I went home. (I did walk off once at Donte's while Jack Sheldon sang "Fuck You Very Much," an unfunny song that begins with the punch line. But I didn't go home; I just sat at the bar until he was finished.)

The next time I saw Anita was ten years later, when I found her sitting at the bar at Donte's. "Mr. Frishberg," she said. "Are we speaking?" I told her, "Not necessarily." (That's the famous line that Lester Lanin uttered when a customer asked, "Are you Jewish?")

Sometimes she would sing well, but that was the exception. I've heard records where she sounds terrific, but drugs and alcohol don't explain why she was so erratic and reckless and unmusical when all she had to do was sing the song and she sounded good. She screwed up all the songs because she couldn't stop acting hip. "Luh-guh-guh-guv for say-gay-gay-gayle." What's that supposed to be? Is it hip to gargle?

Three

Peel Me a Grape

Peel Me a Grape

Peel me a grape
Crush me some ice
Skin me a peach, save the fuzz for my pillow
Start me a smoke
Talk to me nice
You gotta wine me
And dine me
Don't try and train me
Chow mein me
Best way to serve me
Hors d'oeuvre me
I'm getting hungry . . .
Peel me a grape

Pop me a cork
French me a fry
Crack me a nut, bring a bowl fulla bonbons
Chill me some wine
Keep standing by

Just entertain me
Champagne me
Best way to cheer me
Cashmere me
Best way to smell me
Chanel me
I'm getting hungry . . .
Peel me a grape

Here's how to be an agreeable chap
Love me and leave me in luxury's lap
Hop when I holler, skip when I snap
When I say, "Do it,"
Jump to it

Send out for scotch
Call me a cab
Cut me a rose, make my tea with the petals
Just hang around
Pick up the tab
Never outthink me, just mink me
Polar bear rug me, don't bug me

New Thunderbird me
You heard me
I'm getting hungry
Peel me a grape

Words and music by Dave Frishberg
© 1962 Dave Frishberg

The Grape Seed

"Peel Me a Grape," written quickly and carelessly in 1962, was the first song I showed to a publisher, and when I hear it nowadays I always feel like I'm hearing the work of a beginner songwriter.

I was writing all kinds of songs then—folk songs, country songs, novelty songs, grotesque attempts at rock 'n' roll, blues—I knew no shame. I've tried to recall my state of mind in those years, and it strikes me that I wasn't striving for excellence. Instead, I was trying to sound like what I heard on the radio. I was unmindful of the fact that I was writing *down* to the listener. Way down.

I had written a handful of songs with lyrics, but I didn't show them to anybody until my wife Stella introduced me to her friends Alfred Uhry and Bob Waldman, who were writing a Broadway musical. I had never met real songwriters before, and I was fascinated to observe the way they were designing songs for the theater. These guys could write. Alfred, who was the lyric writer, took a look at one of my lyrics one day and said, "Stop trying to make it sound like 'song lyrics.' Forget the 'moonlit magic' bullshit and write simple and straight ahead, like people really talk." Wow. Alfred nailed it. I never felt the same way about lyrics after that.

During a rehearsal, singer Fran Jeffries, who was intensely glamorous, remarked to me that she needed some special material so she could slink around while singing. "Something like 'Whatever Lola Wants,'" she said. I went to work that night and came up with 'Peel Me a Grape.' Next time I saw her I showed her my new song. I said, "How's this for the special material you mentioned the other day?" Fran said, "It's cute. But we decided to put in a fast samba number there. It's a different mood." When I played the grape song for Waldman and Uhry they said, "Show it to Frank Loesser's publishing company. We'll tell Frank you're coming." "You know Frank Loesser?" I said. "Of course we know him," Waldman said. "Who do you think is producing our show? We bring all our songs to Frank Music." Soon after, I took 'Grape' and some other songs to Frank Music on 57th Street. Bert Siegelson and Milt Kramer listened to me demonstrate the songs at the spinet, and soon we had signed contracts for four songs.

A couple of days later, I stopped in at the office and gave them a revised version of "Grape." I had inserted two beats of rest after the word *hungry* each time it occurred. "Please," I told Siegelson and Kramer, "make sure that you don't use the lead sheet I gave you last week. Discard it. Use this revised version when you make the demo." "Of course," said Bert. "No Problem," said Milt. I heard the demo a month later. Guess what. Luckily, I was able to intervene in time to prevent the uncorrected lead sheets and demo tapes from being thrust into the hands of the correct people. Meanwhile, in my piano work I met Fred Karlin, a young trumpet player/composer/arranger, and I had been involved in rehearsing and recording some of his music with small jazz ensembles. One day a contractor called and hired me on a date for Epic Records. John Hammond was the producer; the leader was Fred Karlin. I was quite excited, because these studio calls didn't come my way that often. I had no idea what the music might be.

When I got to the studio I found that the featured artist was Nikki Price, a young singer from Hartford, and we were scheduled to record four titles. I went to the piano and began to look over the parts, and among them was a part for a song called 'Peel Me a Grape.' I took it over to Fred, who was on the conductor's podium and said, "Isn't this a drag? You won't believe this, but I just wrote a song called 'Peel Me a Grape,' and here comes somebody else with the same title." Fred laughed and said, "That's your song. That's why I asked for you. I wanted to see your face when you saw the title." My first reaction was to check my part to make certain the critical two beats rest were being observed. Sure enough, everything was kosher. So Nikki Price made the first recording of the song, and did a very good job. It was the first time one of my songs had been recorded.

It wasn't long before several other singers recorded "Grape," and their albums sold in the dozens. After that, nearly twenty years passed before another recording was made, although I was aware that the song was being performed by female singers in the U.S., Europe, and Asia. Frank Music Company had apparently stuck "Peel Me a Grape" in a file cabinet along with a few other of my songs and, as far as I know, the song was a pretty confidential item until Blossom Dearie's version, recorded at Ronnie Scott's club in London, came out on a British LP.

Diana Krall's Version

Diana Krall's recording of "Peel Me a Grape" in the late '90s was the one that established the song as an internationally known piece of material. When I heard the record, I was impressed by her excellence, but puzzled by her departure from the lyrics. I had written, "Start me a smoke; talk to me nice . . ." and she sang, "Talk to me nice; talk to me nice."

By this time, my publishing company, Swiftwater Music, had acquired from Frank Music all the rights to "Grape." My publisher, David Rosner, called Tommy LiPuma, producer of the Krall date, and cordially wondered about "Talk to me nice, talk to me nice." LiPuma informed David that Krall was passionately against smoking, and didn't want that reference in the lyric. Both Rosner and I felt that was peculiar—but okay, no big deal. Since then I've heard at least a couple of performances of "Grape" in which the singer repeats, "Talk to me nice." It's kind of a drag. But I was never crazy about the lyric anyway.

When I met Krall for the first time I said, "Excuse me, but I'm going outside for a cigarette," expecting I would now hear Diana's anti-tobacco diatribe. But instead she said, "I'll join you." And indeed she did. As we puffed away, I didn't press the matter. After all, it's the closest thing to a big-selling record I've been involved with. I think the producers probably intended to fix the error, then forgot to do so, and LiPuma was embarrassed to admit it. I've since quit smoking, and I hope Diana has too.

By the way, the expression "peel me a grape" was uttered by Mae West in a movie from the early 1930s. That's where I got it, of course. I got "fuzz for my pillow" from an old recording of the vaudeville team called Moran and Mack. I know no shame.

Cut Me a Check

Re: Licensing "PMGrape" for Banana Republic TV ads
To: David Rosner, Bicycle Music

"Peel Me a Grape" is the fourth installment in an ongoing television campaign for Banana Republic. The merchandise is cashmere, the subject is luxury, or rather poking fun at the idea of luxury. The song, which is an old cabaret classic, will be used in a new modern way, as a male-female duet (Blossom Dearie and Lyle Lovett) in which Lyle gets his share of the "you've got to wine me and dine me" lyrics. Images of people wearing cashmere while "pampering" each other in funny or tender ways will be intercut with interesting pieces of stock footage based on how they connect to the shots and convey the feeling of cashmere.

Creative Director

Rosner to Frishberg: I have no problem with this. You?
Frishberg to Rosner: No problemo
Slip me a peel, make me a deal

Send me the cash, pay the bills with bananas
Talk to me nice. Say the line twice
It wouldn't hoit me, exploit me.
Blossom and Lyle me, defile me
Change and reverse me, imburse me
I'm really easy. . . . Cut me a check.

Sideman for a Singer

Accompanying singers is like being a sideman in a way. Young pianists have asked me for tips about how to polish their skills as accompanists. I can't think of anything to say.

"Stay below middle C"? I've been told that's what Peggy Lee would tell a new accompanist. I've never been deliberately conscious of that restriction while I'm playing, although I often find myself on that side of the keyboard to keep things mellow. All things considered, it depends on the music you're playing, but it's a sensible thought to keep in mind.

I think of Ted Williams's famous quote when a reporter asked him to identify the key element in becoming a proficient batter. Williams answered without hesitation, "Get a good pitch to hit." I feel the same about learning to be an effective accompanist: "Get a good singer."

Three varieties of good singers:

1. Singer knows exactly what the accompaniment should sound like. The singer hears that ideal accompaniment while singing. It's up to you to match it. Good luck.
2. Singer responds to the extemporaneous accompaniment you provide. This can be fun and musically rewarding. Be wary of scat singers, and don't encourage them.

3. Singer plows ahead correctly, not missing a note, while you are floundering trying to play "Lush Life" in E. It's okay to say, "I need to practice this."

Rehearsals can be the most enjoyable part of the gig, but both singer and accompanist will know in a flash after the first few bars whether this relationship is headed for smooth sailing or utter doom. The good singers sing good with or without you.

Benny Goodman

My first meeting with Goodman was at a rehearsal of his big band—I was subbing for the regular pianist (Russ Freeman)—in 1960 maybe, at Nola studios on Broadway. I remember Roy Burns was the drummer, and rehearsers that day included Freddy Greenwell, Zoot Sims, Marky Markowitz, Jerry Dodgion, Tommy Newsom, Bill Crow, et al. My knees were rubbery of course.

Benny called number twenty-five and I found myself staring at an Eddie Sauter "concerto" with Mel Powell's piano solo and fills transcribed in the piano part. I tried to grab an eyeful of the first four bars so I could at least start with the band, and suddenly Benny was counting off. The band was playing something not remotely related to my part.

Benny cut them off. "Ready, piano?" he said. We tried it again—same train wreck. Benny stood next to me with his clarinet and instructed me to play the chart alone with him. It was a nightmare, a total humiliation, a disaster, and we stopped after about eight bars. The guys in the band were looking off in five different directions.

Benny said, "That sounds about right," and counted off the band again. Their music still had nothing to do with my part. He stopped the band and called to me, "Hey Pops, what number you got up?"

My parents, Harry and Sarah, on their wedding day.
(Personal collection)

With my brothers, Arnold and Morton. (Personal collection)

Eighth grade at Groveland Park Elementary School, St. Paul, Minnesota, in 1946.
I am standing in the front row, sixth from the left. (Personal collection)

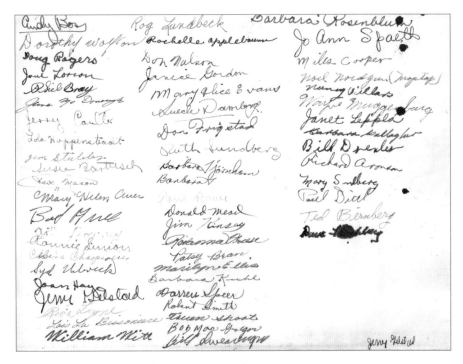

My signature is the last one. (Personal collection)

As a child, I spent hours daily drawing comics and comic strips and thought I'd do it for a living. Little did I know then that I'd become a professional musician. (Personal collection)

Some of my drawings of baseball players. (Personal collection)

Smilin' Stan Hack, third baseman for the Chicago Cubs in the late '30s and early '40s. (Personal collection)

Publicity photograph of the Rollie Anfinson Combo, taken at the Sigma Chi house at the University of Minnesota, circa 1951. Dick Zemlin, a trumpet player, posed with a saxophone because Rollie didn't show up. (Personal collection)

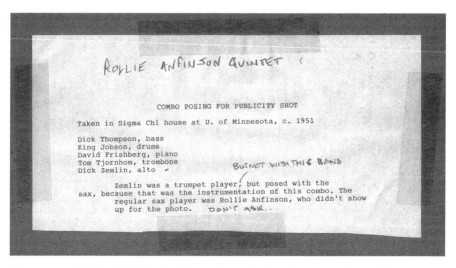

ROLLIE ANFINSON QUINTET

COMBO POSING FOR PUBLICITY SHOT

Taken in Sigma Chi house at U. of Minnesota, c. 1951

Dick Thompson, bass
King Jobson, drums
David Frishberg, piano
Tom Tjornhom, trombone
Dick Zemlin, alto — BUT NOT WITH THIS BAND

    Zemlin was a trumpet player, but posed with the
sax, because that was the instrumentation of this combo. The
    regular sax player was Rollie Anfinson, who didn't show
up for the photo. DON'T ASK..

My notes on the back of the Rollie Anfinson Combo photo. (Personal collection)

With the Bob Kunin Band at Hillcrest Country Club, St. Paul, 1953. (Personal collection)

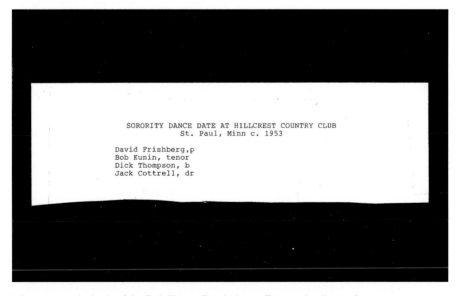

My notes on the back of the Bob Kunin Band photo. (Personal collection)

Administering oaths to female air force enlistees. (Personal collection)

My official U.S. Air Force photograph, taken July 20, 1955. (Personal collection)

Administering oaths to male air force enlistees. (Personal collection)

USAF officers in Utah. I'm seated in the front row, second from the left. (Personal collection)

I'm standing next to a USAF training plane in San Angelo, TX. I had to fly in this aircraft as part of my training. (Personal collection)

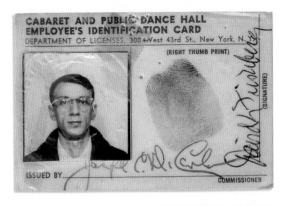

Finally made it in New York City. My cabaret card, issued on September 30, 1965. (Personal collection)

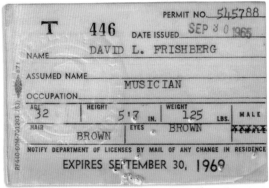

The back of my NYC cabaret card. (Personal collection)

Zoot Sims and Al Cohn practicing in the Poconos, my former home, in November 1978. (Garth Woods)

"Twenty-five," I told him.

"No, Pops, no. I said forget twenty-five. We're playing number nineteen. Try to pay attention."

I survived the rest of the rehearsal without major mishaps. But that wasn't the end. A month later I still hadn't been paid for the rehearsal. I called Jay Feingold, Goodman's business manager, and reminded him about the payment. Feingold agreed to send a check to the union, and I said thanks. An hour later Feingold called back, "Dave? Benny says he never told you he'd pay you for that rehearsal." I said, "I signed a withholding slip at the studio." "I'll take care of it," Feingold said, and a couple of weeks later I picked up the check at the union and discovered that Benny Goodman had been quibbling about a paycheck for twelve dollars.

∼

In 1962 I was playing with Gene Krupa's quartet at the Metropole in Times Square. One night Benny Goodman walked in and the place went crazy. We were on the bandstand, just having finished an hour-and-fifteen-minute set. I looked at Gene and his face was white. He says, "It's the King of Swing, and he's got his horn. I don't believe this. Here he comes."

So Benny walked up on the stand and began to try out reeds. He sat on a high bar stool, staring off into space, and tootled and fluttered up and down the scale. This went on for long minutes. Meanwhile, Jack Waldorf, the Metropole manager, had herded dozens—hundreds—of passersby into the club, and he had them chanting, "Benny! Benny!" Some were hollering out years—like "1936!" The camera girl, standing down by the bar, snapped a picture, and hurried downstairs to make prints, promising photos for Goodman and Krupa to sign.

Benny was finally ready. He said, "Brushes, Gene." Remember, this was Gene's band. Gene obediently picked up the brushes and flashed a big smile, but I could see he was in a cold fury. Then Benny turned to me and said, "'Sweet Lorraine' in G. Give me a little introduction." I complied, and Benny entered in F. He waved me out and finished his solo without piano.

We stayed on the stand for about an hour. The camera girl was going into a second printing. Then, abruptly, Goodman packed up his horn and descended, demanding safe escort through the crowd, and he was gone into the night. He hadn't signed one picture. Krupa was drenched with two shows' worth of perspiration, but he sat patiently on the steps of the bandstand and signed dozens of photos. I saw that he was writing personal notes on each one, and he was asking each customer, "Who shall I inscribe this to?"

Later, in the dressing room, Gene said to us, "I was glad to sign this picture. This will be in a lot of homes, believe me. Did you get a load of this?" We inspected the picture then. And there was Benny with his horn in his mouth, perched on a stool with his legs spread wide. His fly was wide open; two buttons showed plainly. "Buttons!" Gene said. "Buttons! That suit's probably from about 1940."

∼

Speaking of clothes: Sol Yaged drove me home from the Metropole late one night, and down around Seventh Avenue and 33rd he stopped the car at the curb and pointed to a high window in an office building. "That's where Benny buys his suits," he said quietly.

∼

Once, Ruby Braff brought Benny to a jam session at Marshall Brown's studio. Naturally, a chill fell over the room as the two of them walked in. Benny took nearly an hour to find a reed, and the rest of us had to wait, couldn't play because he was noodling with a dozen different reeds, and wouldn't stop. Finally we played a tune, "On the Alamo," and Benny took every chorus, interrupting the other players in mid-chorus, and then conducted the ending. I left and don't know what happened after that.

~

In California, some years later, maybe 1975, my song "I'm Hip" was to be performed by Mitzi Gaynor in her TV special, and several days before the taping I learned that Benny Goodman would be joining her on the vocal. I persuaded Dick DeBenedictis, the musical director, to let me visit the set. I promised I would keep my mouth shut.

They had a very hip little band to accompany Benny on the show, including John Bunch, Jack Sheldon, and Frank Rosolino. Tommy Newsom had written a nice arrangement of "I'm Hip" for Gaynor and Goodman. On the run-through, Mitzi sang it perfectly, but there was confusion on Benny's first vocal entrance, which occurred on the pickup to the bridge. Benny was coming in a bar late.

Dick DeBenedictis said, "Benny, you have a three-beat pickup there: 'Every Saturday night.' The word *night* is the downbeat—anticipated."

"Gotcha, Pops," said Benny. They ran through it again. Benny made the same mistake, but he assured Dick that he understood. "Let's roll, then," said the director, and the taping began. Mitzi Gaynor sailed through, but when Benny's entrance came, he again waited a bar too long, and the taping ground to a stop. DeBenedictis explained patiently that Benny had to sing three beats pickup before the downbeat of the bridge. "You're going to have to count there, Benny," he said. Benny squinted at him and said, "Say, Pops, aren't we getting a little fussy?"

They went on from there, Benny fluffing a vocal entrance or two, and the band expertly accommodating his "mistakes." I was puzzled, because it seemed that Goodman was making things awkward deliberately, and I couldn't imagine why he would want to do such a thing, except to demonstrate his prerogative to behave that way.

He certainly did play masterfully, and he could swing his tail off. But gimme a break.

Jack Fine's Cinderella Band

Cornetist Jack Fine had a steady weekend at the Cinderella Club in the Village, c. 1961–'62. I was often playing piano—a sixty-six-key job—the rest of the band was usually Joe Muranyi on clarinet, Marshall Brown on valve trombone, Al McManus on drums, and Ahmed Abdul-Malik on bass. We used to hang in the basement between sets, smoking cigarettes and drinking wine that we brought in from a nearby store.

Everyone in the band was pretty strange and intense—a reflection of its leader. Jack was a passionate and dramatic cornet player. He played his heart out on every tune, as if it were his last chance at it. I have some tapes that I made at the Cinderella on my old Tandberg, and Jack sounds terrific, in the Armstrong mode via Ruby Braff and Wild Bill Davison.

George Wettling played one night, followed us down into the basement, unzipped his pants, and, with a cigarette dangling from his lips, proceeded to pee into a sink. I shot a questioning look at Muranyi, who shrugged and reminded me that Wettling was a terrific drummer, and indeed he was.

Marshall Brown couldn't take off his music teacher's hat, and shouted things at us, like "Tag!" or "E-flat seventh!" And during ensembles he would aim his horn right into your face and try to teach you the tune by playing the trombone part. Off the stand, Marshall and I would crack up when we listened to the jukebox and heard the grotesque confections that were currently the rage. Marshall would grab my arm, make his eyes bulge, and chant into my face: "'Duke Duke Duke Duke of Earl Duke Duke Duke of Earl Duke Duke!' Is that a lyric or what? What does it mean? What does it mean?" One night I told him, "If you have to ask, you'll never know."

Jack Fine had created an identity for himself: mysterious beatnik with secrets. He always had some attractive starched coed from Pembroke or Vassar on his arm, and he wouldn't introduce her to anyone. We would joke about how Jack was offering these innocent girls a titillating glimpse of the dark side of jazz by bringing them into the Cinderella. I returned to the club late one night to retrieve something and found Jack in shirtsleeves stacking the chairs and mopping the floor while Betsy Bennington waited patiently on a bar stool. Jack sheepishly informed me that this was part of his agreement with the Cinderella. I suggested "Mop Mop" for the band's theme song. Got a laugh.

Gene Krupa

I was with Gene's quartet during the years 1962–'64. We didn't make any major trips, but stuck close to home on the East Coast, playing weekend dates in nearby New Jersey, Pennsylvania, and Maryland. And of course we worked the Metropole in NYC regularly, sometimes for two or three weeks at a time.

During that time, Eddie Wasserman was the saxophonist and Kenny O'Brien, Dave Perlman, or Bill Takas played bass. Charlie Ventura took Wasserman's place on at least one occasion—our two-week engagement at the Steel Pier, Atlantic City, August of 1962. Years later in a London record store, I picked up an LP that contains radio broadcasts we did on that gig.

I must say that I never had much of a personal friendship with Gene, although our relationship was cordial throughout the period. My impression of him is that he was a very kind, thoughtful man, and extremely moral and ethical, quite religious—at least he always made a point of attending Mass on Sunday morning. I was surprised to find him that way, considering his public image as a hopped-up dope fiend.

We younger members of the band were not that concerned with rectitude. Gene never hung out with us, never smoked pot with us, and I understood from the very beginning that he couldn't afford to be compromised in any way. He intimated that the police—especially in the small towns—would like nothing better than to bust Gene Krupa and get some local notoriety.

I don't remember seeing Gene take so much as a drink while we were on the job. He was always sharp and alert and ready to perform. *The Gene Krupa Story* was playing currently, and I went to see it and laughed at the scene where the Krupa character drops his sticks during the big solo, and the audience realizes that he's "back on the stuff." I remember at least a couple of occasions in real life when Gene dropped a stick, and people in the audience began whispering among themselves and pointing at Gene.

In the car driving to and from gigs, he would search the radio for baseball broadcasts, especially the Chicago White Sox, if they were within radio range. He was a rabid Sox fan. He listened with intense concentration, and there wasn't much conversation with the passengers in the car. Once in the car he reminisced about the Austin High School group in Chicago and their assortment of bohemian friends, characters we would call "beatniks" in later years. There were avid readers among them, and the English humorists were favored. Gene remembered Bud Freeman, Bix Beiderbecke, Dave Tough, and others quoting dialog from P. G. Wodehouse. Gene said his own favorite was *Three Men in a Boat* by Jerome K. Jerome. He said Bix could quote long passages from that book.

Gene finally found it necessary to fire me. He was very polite when he explained it to me. "You're a very good player, but you're forgetting one thing," he said. "This is my band, not yours, and I want it to sound the way I like, not the way you like." I was hurt at the time, because I thought I was doing the best job possible, and actually making the group sound "better."

A few years later I had a better perspective on many things, including that incident, and I was able to understand how Gene felt about my playing—I was, after all, supposed to be his accompanist, and it was his name, not mine, that was on the marquee and drawing people in. And if I'm forced to consider my shortcomings as an ensemble player, I must admit I tend to be "pushy" and opinionated about how the music should sound. It's not much fun for me to play a subdued, anonymous role in the rhythm section. Gene couldn't tolerate that, and obviously didn't need that kind of competition in the band. He knew exactly what he wanted to hear and how he wanted it to feel, and if it didn't agree with my musical instincts, well, that was my tough luck. We parted friends, but I could feel that Gene was trying to teach me a lesson. And that was only fair, considering that I'd been trying to teach him one all along, from the piano.

Ben Webster

It was the summer of 1963 when I joined Ben Webster's quartet. He was playing at the Shalimar on Seventh Avenue near 123rd Street. I couldn't believe I got the call, because I had never met Ben or even seen him in the flesh, and I was told that he hadn't heard me play. Here's how it all came about:

I used to play in rehearsal bands at Lynn Oliver's studio on Broadway and 81st. I met the great saxophone player Joe Henderson at one of these rehearsals, and he invited me to play a jam session job on the East Side on a Sunday afternoon. Kenny Dorham was the leader, Henderson on tenor, Al Foster drums, and Ray McKinney on bass. McKinney was new in town from Detroit, and he told me he was about to start a nightly job with Ben Webster in Harlem.

A couple nights later, McKinney phoned me and told me that Ben Webster wanted to replace the piano player on the new gig. Ben had agreed to "audition" me on the gig—could I make it tonight? I said of course, and I quickly put on a suit and tie, dashed out into a furious rainstorm, and grabbed a subway up to Harlem.

Ben was very cordial, and after the first set, I thanked him, and Ben said, "Don't go anywhere. You got the gig." I was thrilled, and I told Ray McKinney how excited I was and thanked him for proposing me. The next night McKinney was gone, replaced by Richard Davis, and I don't think our paths ever crossed again.

So the rhythm section turned out to be me, Richard Davis, and Mel Lewis, and that was among the most comfortable situations in my experience. When the Shalimar gig ended and we began to play around at different clubs in New York, Richard stayed on but Mel Lewis left, and several drummers were involved after that.

I kept a journal of my jobs for tax purposes, and I can reconstruct my employment record with Ben from those notes, but I neglected to write down the venues and personnel. And of course there were casual jobs that were cash transactions, and I kept no record of those. But here's what I can come up with (dates are questionable, personnel is from memory).

Ben Webster Gigs

(Drummers noted. Except as noted, Richard Davis was on bass on all these)

1963

July 6–8	Shalimar	$90	Mel Lewis
July 9–14	Shalimar	$140	Mel Lewis
July 15–21	Shalimar	$140	Mel Lewis
July 22–28	Shalimar	$140	Mel Lewis
August 8	Town Hall	$100	Art Davis, bass; Elvin Jones, drums
August 13–18	Half Note	$150	Mel Lewis
August 20–25	Half Note	$150	Mel Lewis
September 17–22	Half Note	$150	Mel Lewis, Philly Joe Jones, Grady Tate
September 23–29	Half Note	$150	Grady Tate
November 1–7	Birdland	$150	Denzil Best
November 8–13	Birdland	$150	Denzil Best

1964

February 1–6	Village Vanguard	$150	Mickey Roker
February 7–13	Café au Go Go (opp. George Carlin)	$150	Jackie Williams

Ben was very emotional and his feelings were close to the surface. I knew that Ben was famous for unpredictable outbursts of anger and violence, but I never saw him pull any of those stunts, perhaps because he was trying to abstain from hard liquor at that time. He did drink beer—Rheingold. When he drank he was quick to weep. He would ask Richard to play solos with the bow, and then he would stand listening, with tears rolling down his cheeks. He would get tearful when he spoke of his mother. Once he told me that he missed Jimmy Rowles, who was back in California, and as he told me about his friendship with Rowles he began to cry. One night at the Half Note we heard radio reports of rioting in Harlem, and Ben wept openly as he listened.

I visited Ben in his hotel room and also at the apartment he shared with Joe Zawinul. He always had tapes playing—mostly Art Tatum records and Ellington from the 1930s and '40s. He made me a dub (reel-to-reel) of the famous Duke Ellington Fargo, North Dakota, concert that featured Webster and Jimmy Blanton. He loved Tatum, Fats Waller, James P. Johnson—knew all the stride moves on the piano, and he could execute "Carolina Shout" and some of those pieces at very slow tempo. He could tell from my playing that I was influenced in that direction, and that pleased him, because he was a fan and admirer of that music.

I think Ben got some heat from black musicians because he included me (and Mel Lewis) in his band. Ben was protective of both of us. During the Shalimar engagement Ben took me and Mel next door to the little grocery store where he knew the proprietor. He introduced us to the man, who assured us that we could take refuge in his store if it ever became necessary. I didn't even know what he was talking about.

When we played the Half Note, an obnoxious guy at the bar asked Ben to play "Danny Boy," and Ben was gruff in his reply: "We already played that." The stranger at the bar took offense and began to insist, "Well, play it again!" Ben began to get sassy with him, and the customer turned out to be a cop. He flashed his NYPD badge and instructed Ben to get off the stage. The cop took him outside, and we followed behind to see what was going to happen. Ben had his palms up against the wall, and the cop was patting him down and hassling him. The Canterino family, proprietors of the Half Note, came out, Frank from the kitchen, and his sons Sonny and Mike from behind the bar, and they calmed everybody down including the cop, who seemed to be drunk. I was pretty shaken by the whole episode, and I was impressed to see how the Canterinos handled the cop by quietly talking to him. The guy was apparently impressed by the Canterinos' reasoning, because he backed off and left the premises. Ben didn't feel like playing after that. Richie Kamuca was there, and he unpacked his saxophone and finished the set with us.

Ben spoke of Ellington with the utmost respect and admiration, and referred to his experience with the Ellington band as his "university education." He escorted me and my wife Stella to an Ellington rehearsal at Basin Street East, and introduced us to Ellington. "This is my piano player," he told Duke, "and he can play." Duke said, "You better play if you're in Ben's band." Ben once told me that I was one of the few pianists he'd heard that could emulate Ellington's time feeling. I was thrilled to get such a compliment.

Many great musicians came into the Shalimar and the Half Note to see Ben, and they often brought their horns. I got a chance to play with Johnny Hodges, Paul Gonsalves, Ray Nance, Lockjaw Davis, and others. Billy Strayhorn came in one night and asked me, "Would it be all right if I played a tune or two?" I stood by and watched him play with the band. It was one of those moments. I was happy to be in New York, and privileged to be a musician, consorting with these giants. When Al Cohn and Zoot Sims heard us at the Shalimar, they took me aside and hired me for their upcoming New York dates, and thus began a relationship that lasted until I left New York about nine years later.

Me and Malcolm

In July 1963 I joined Ben Webster's quartet at the Shalimar, on Seventh Avenue and 123rd Street, across the street from the Hotel Theresa. The Theresa was headquarters for Elijah Muhammad and the Black Muslim movement. The clientele at the Shalimar was practically all black, and it often seemed like drummer Mel Lewis and I were the only white males for blocks around. I felt a definite chill in the air, especially around the Fruit of Islam guys in their sharp navy-blue suits, but people were polite, maybe because they saw we were with Ben Webster and Ben was a big hero in that neighborhood.

There was a group of four or five well-dressed men who sometimes hung out at a table near the far corner of the bar. They would be in deep conversation, and never glanced at me when I waited to order from the bartender. It sounded like they were into politics and world affairs, but I didn't pay much attention. One night I overheard them trying to name the Detroit Tigers infield from 1934, and they were stuck at third base. So I said, "How about Marvin Owen?" And this one guy turned to me and we began to fire names at each other: Billy Sullivan, Dick Bartell, Johnny Gorsica, Elon Hogsett, and on and on for a few minutes, and then it was time for me to go back on the bandstand. Ben said to me, "You know who you're talking to over there?" I said I didn't and he said, "Ever heard of Malcolm X?" I said, "No kidding!" and that was that.

We stayed at the Shalimar for the rest of the summer. One night I was standing with some people out in front of the club smoking a cigarette, and I saw Malcolm and his friends coming across the street from the hotel. As Malcolm passed by he gave me a smile and said, "Hey, baseball!" I don't remember who I was standing with, but they looked at me with new respect. "You know him?" "Of course," I replied.

Al and Zoot at the Half Note
Liner Essay for Verve Reissue of 1960 LP *You'n'Me*, the Al Cohn-Zoot Sims Quintet

Al Cohn and Zoot Sims? Together and separately they were probably the most widely admired musicians I ever came across. I used to watch other musicians listen to them, and I remember how their faces would light up, and how they would burst into spontaneous cheering and howling. I think it might have been the drummer Jake Hanna who said, "Everybody wants to either play like Zoot and talk like Al or play like Al and talk like Zoot." And back in the days when these recordings were made, Stan Getz was being widely quoted as saying that his dream tenor player would have "my sound, Zoot Sims's time, and Al Cohn's ideas." I recently heard another great saxophonist, Phil Woods, comment during a radio interview that something "ain't the big leagues . . . it ain't Zoot and Al."

When I got to New York in search of the big leagues in the late '50s I began attending the jam sessions that went on night and day in David X. Young's loft on Sixth Avenue. The music was hot, and the cast of characters was fabulous. You never knew who might wander in. That's when I first met Al Cohn and Zoot Sims. They arrived together one night, with their horns of course, but also bearing about a gallon of Neapolitan ice cream, which we helped them demolish. I remember sitting there mentally pinching myself; I was about to play with Zoot Sims, man, and Al Cohn! But they never unpacked their horns. They presently got up and left, and

I never got to play with either of them until a few years later, in 1963, when I joined their band at the Half Note.

In the play *Sideman* there's a heart-stopping moment where the trumpet player's wife sits in a near empty nightclub admiring her husband's inspired playing. She turns to her friend and says, "He sounds so great. Do you think he's ever going to make it?," and the friend says happily, "What do you mean make it? This is it. He's made it!" Any musician in the audience could identify with that line. I thought of the Half Note.

Not that the Half Note was an empty nightclub. It was a flourishing family-operated Italian restaurant in the warehouse and factory district south of the Village. The music was not only hot, but it was currently fashionable, it was popular, it was relevant. The musicians weren't playing "oldies" or trying to "re-create" anything. It was the current music of the day, and I felt like I was a part of it, although it was unsettling to contemplate the pop music revolution all too apparent on the horizon. The customers were still young adults, people my age, and they celebrated the music and were loyal to it. It was hip to like jazz in those days, and to me the Half Note seemed like the hippest place in town. Sometimes I'd catch myself thinking, "This is it. You've made it."

If you were a piano player doing jazz work in New York in those years, you couldn't ask for a more nourishing, more rewarding experience than to play with Al and Zoot. In the first place, you got to hang with Al and Zoot and their colleagues and friends and fans at the Half Note every night. You got to play with Jimmy Rushing on the weekends. And $90 a week wasn't bad, especially if you supplemented it by rehearsing a singer or two. The point was that you could be involved, you could be included, you could be on the scene each night making hot music with two immortals in their prime. This was Zoot 'n' Al, man! This was jazz playing of the highest order and purity, the most serious and sublime joy. This was why you came to New York.

At the Half Note the music took place in the middle of the room, on a high narrow platform in back of the bar. Sonny and Mike Canterino poured drinks and punched the cash register directly beneath the musicians, and when the bar action quieted they would sometimes stand and look up at the players with big, beaming smiles.

During the bass solo, Al Cohn would drain the contents of a shot glass in one gulp, then, staring straight ahead, he would hold the glass with thumb and index finger at arm's length, shoulder level, and let it drop. Sonny or Mike would whirl and pluck the glass cleanly out of the air with barely a glance upward. Mousey Alexander would "catch" the action with a cymbal crash. I never saw anybody miss. The customers told each other, "Now that's hip. That's class."

And they were right, of course. I felt the same way. The shtick with the shot glass seemed to express the unflappable comic worldliness that was Al Cohn's personal magic. But it went deeper than that. When Al and Zoot played, they spoke straight to the music in each of us, player and listener alike. Somebody once remarked that when Zoot Sims starts to play, everything starts to sound better. I agreed and reminded him that Al Cohn need only enter the room to make it happen. What a thrill, what a privilege, to be on the stand with them.

These 1960 recordings by the relatively new Cohn/Sims quintet represent the group as they appeared at the Half Note near the beginning of their long association with that famous nightclub. Al and Zoot are in typical big-league form. In "The Note," I hear Al

Cohn nailing down the time his way, and then Zoot enters with his solo and, like flipping a light switch, he shows us a different way of generating a swing feeling. And Al is typically droll, beginning his solo with a Stravinsky quote. We get a taste of pianist Mose Allison, whose graceful comping and soloing sounds like nobody else. The way he articulates the time and glides from note to note (as in his solo on "The Opener") is so personal that Allison the instrumentalist is practically impossible to imitate. And that goes for Major Holley too, who was a champion ensemble player besides being a unique soloist. I'm not sure whether Osie Johnson was at the Half Note, though. He wasn't doing a lot of nightclub work; he was far too busy in the studios.

And talk about tight schedules: Remember, these were the years when Al Cohn maintained a parallel career as one of the busiest arrangers in New York, writing around the clock, churning out charts for TV specials, Broadway scores, and studio recordings. In later years, as Al's eyesight began to grow weaker, he withdrew from the arranging marathon and remarked that he was relieved and grateful in a way, because he could now "devote some time to the saxophone." Then we saw him grow into an even more powerful and profound player than he had been before. When the beatnik jazz musicians of my generation reminisce they (we) usually get to the Al Cohn stories and Zoot Sims quotes, because Al and Zoot were funny, they were always "on," and they constellated laughter wherever they were. New Year's Eve 1965 during a radio broadcast from the Half Note, when they counted down to midnight Zoot began to play "Happy Birthday," and when the announcer stopped him and corrected him, Zoot apologized and said amiably, "I knew it was something festive." And it was at the Half Note that a customer gushed, "Zoot, you're amazing. Even when you're drunk you sound great. How do you pull it off?" and Zoot shot back deadpan, "I practice drunk," and walked away.

I used to think that everyone's secret desire must be to talk and act like Al Cohn, who was my model (everyone's model?) for how an artist and a gentleman should behave. Al had his own brand of good-natured dark humor. One night we finished at the Half Note, and Zoot didn't want to stop. The customers were gone, Mousey was packing up the drums, and Zoot was alone on the bandstand, wailing away chorus after chorus of "Stompin' at the Savoy" or something like that. Al was standing at the bar with his coat and hat on, and he yelled, "Zoot! Take off the red shoes!" That tickled me. I'll never forget it. "Take off the red shoes!" You had to be there, I guess. Well, listening to this music takes me back there, which is okay because—let's face it— the past is home to me. It's home to me and the other surviving musicians from Zoot and Al's generation, and I speculate on how quaint we must seem now to the younger people who have never been interested in the music we play. We're the guys with the half-diminished chords and tri-tone substitutions who know "all the tunes" and like to talk about swinging. We're today's "old-time" musicians, like the polka-band musicians of my childhood. And just like Whoopee John or the Six Fat Dutchmen or Frankie Yankovic, we're keeping alive the music of the "old country," except that unlike those polka guys, we come from various racial and national backgrounds, and the term *old country* no longer refers to some place overseas.

(Later, I added additional material.)

And talk about a cast of characters: Among the steady customers, especially during the late closing hours, you could count on seeing the regular neighborhood "faces," like Big Dick the giant longshoreman, and his king-size girlfriend Loretta, who both towered over all of us, and Honest John Annen, a glum and silent man, who, if he spoke at all, spoke in riddles or mysterious monosyllables. I can remember entire conversations with him, lasting several minutes, and often becoming quite heated, during which I understood not one sentence he spoke or one reference he made. I used to ponder over what he might mean, or what he could possibly be suggesting, until I finally realized that the poor guy was probably schizophrenic. It didn't hit me until years later.

Usually, the last customer out the door was Mister George. George was his first name, nobody asked his last, and he seemed to take a certain pleasure in hearing himself addressed as Mister George. He normally arrived after midnight, after his shift at the Christopher Street post office, and he always sat at the far end of the bar, opposite the kitchen doors, and opposite me, the piano bench being at that end of the stage. After a drink or two, Mister George's forehead would rest on the bar, and his arms would hang down at his sides. He would then stay in that position for the rest of the night, listening with intense concentration to the music, and when something especially worthwhile took place on the bandstand, he would signify his approval by making the "thumbs-up" sign with both hands, while his forehead never left the bar. Al Cohn wrote a piece for the quintet and titled it "Mister George," and when we premiered it at the Half Note, Mister George gave us extravagant thumbs-up signals all during the performance. He never admitted as much, but we could all tell that he was touched and made proud by Al's gesture.

In the days when melody ruled jazz, Zoot Sims was on fire with the melodies of the gods and they flamed out of his horn with such heat that he could swing the whole band into bad health, as people used to say, and bring you off your bar stool.

Al Cohn played like a professor with muscles, and he could chain together fabulous melodic lines that were fresh and coherent. He could deliver his music to you with such confidence and authority, and with such awesome sound and passion that it would bring you to your knees.

During their solos, even if they had too much to drink, they continued to compose as they played—they couldn't help it. They were compulsive composers, and it would be totally out of character for either of them to play reflexive licks, or to quote from nursery rhymes or corny pop songs, or to trivialize their music in any way.

Jazz critics can probably point to certain "influences" in Al's playing, or Zoot's—Lester Young is the obvious point of departure for both players. But the fire and the swing, and the way they swarmed over the changes and discovered ever fresher and more lyrical ways to navigate the songs resembles nothing else that came before or followed after. Al and Zoot each evolved his own musical ethic, his own point of view about improvising, and the way I see it, their music represents the culmination of the musical insights that Lester Young and Charlie Parker and others brought to the dance band musicians in the '30s and '40s. It was basically the Kansas City approach to jazz music, I would suggest, refined, rethought, and resolved into a highly sophisticated musical language. Anyway, all such speculations aside, it was music for adults.

They were both natural blues players, and they played the blues as beautifully as any player I ever heard. I guess you could say Zoot liked to trill, and Al liked to moan; but neither man operated out of a bag of licks. It was not typical of either man to lapse into reflexive or absentminded playing. Their distinctive styles grew out of their compulsive spontaneous melodic invention. And that kind of playing is beyond the reach of most jazz musicians at all levels of accomplishment, including many of the great virtuosos and historical influences of jazz. Musicians like Al and Zoot could pluck melodies out of the trees.

Re: Rowles

I recognized early on in my piano-playing life that there are certain pianists (and I'm talking about jazz players in this discussion) that can touch the keyboard in such a personal way that the informed listener, upon hearing a few notes on a recording, knows instantly who is playing; and I also recognized the remarkable fact that among these pianists, there are a handful who draw such a personal sound out of the keyboard that nobody can duplicate it.

For instance, Duke Ellington can strike a three-note chord in the middle of the piano along with a single note down in the bass, and you can walk up to the same piano and hit the same four notes and you can't get Duke's sound. Blossom Dearie can play a chord and it will sound unearthly quiet, and you can play the same voicing, and it will be beautiful, but it won't sound like Blossom. Often it's the time feeling that's so personal, as with Mose Allison or Erroll Garner or Pete Johnson, but the scary ones are the pianists that can touch a piano key and make a sound that nobody else can make.

Continuing the list of unique sound generators: Count Basie, Eddie Heywood, Claude Thornhill, Nat Cole, Thelonious Monk, Mel Powell, Bud Powell—and outside of the strictly jazz realm don't forget Frankie Carle and Chico Marx. And then there is Jimmy Rowles.

Jimmy Rowles was unique in a different way. It was the way he proceeded from note to note. He spun passages that were so dynamically constructed that he seemed to be bending notes, and everyone knows that's impossible with a piano. Rowles could milk sound from the bass clef register that was almost organ-like. He splashed chords down with a rolling-wristed technique that was his alone. I've never heard anybody come close to his piano sound.

I think he has been my main piano influence, even though I long ago stopped trying to sound like him. I was a teenager in the late '40s when I first heard him on the Woody Herman "Woodchopper" Columbia records. I was stunned by the way he handled his parts in the rhythm section and the sometimes startling way he comped behind soloists. Then I bought the Peggy Lee ten-inch Decca LP *Black Coffee,* and I heard Rowles as accompanist. For my money, nobody touches him when it comes to playing behind singers. His imagination is outrageous, and his taste is flawless—a perfect model for artistic playing.

A couple of decades later, when Jimmy and I had become friends in L.A, I told him what an impact his musicality had on me when I was young. Jimmy was quiet for a moment; then he said, "I notice you've been playing a lot of solo piano lately." He took me over to the piano and showed me some Ellington voicings that opened up my ears and changed my playing in a big way, especially when playing without bass and drums. Jimmy wasn't exactly a teacher, but he could spot what my instincts were, and he knew he could help me. It took less than ten minutes, and I'm still contemplating the insights that Jimmy pointed out.

Once in St. Paul when I was about nineteen, a trumpet player said to me, "Hey, you sound like Jimmy Rowles." Although it wasn't true of course, and it never would be true, I still consider it the most generous and rewarding compliment I ever received. But "sound like Jimmy Rowles"? Forget it.

Four

I Want to Be a Sideman

I Want to Be a Sideman

I want to be a sideman
Just an ordinary sideman
A go along for the ride man
Responsibility free

I want to fill behind the vocal, double on flute,
And jam on the blues
I want to go and join the local, buy a dark suit,
And start paying dues

I want to maintain my book in neatly numbered order
I want to listen to Lester Young on my recorder

I want to play while the people dance
I want to press my own coat and pants
I want to ask for an advance
I want to be a sideman.

II
I want to be a sideman
Just a highly qualified man
A professional pride man
Old indispensable me

Now I can cut whatever comes up, fake and transpose,
and won't make a fuss
I want to set the vibes and drums up, sight-read the shows,
And sleep on the bus

I want to spend all my time with music and musicians
I want to go out and grab a smoke on intermissions

I want to sleep in the afternoons
And let the leader call all the tunes
I want to be young, I want to have fun
I want to be a sideman

I want to work for a superstar
I want to hang in the hotel bar
I want to be young, I want to have fun
I want to be a sideman

Words and music by Dave Frishberg
©1984 Swiftwater Music

The Song Is Me

As you may notice from scanning the printed lyrics, this song is constructed in ABCD form. That's when the melodic content of each section (or stanza) is different, and the sections don't recur. The conventional pop songs of the classic era were written in AABA form—two statements of A, then a contrasting statement (called a "bridge"), which is B, and then another statement of A—often expanded for the coda. Many composers of that period occasionally employed the ABCD form, sometimes called a "through-composed" melodic line, but I think of Irving Berlin ("All Alone"; "God Bless America") as being especially attracted to that method. That's why I think of this song as "my Irving Berlin song."

My friend the late Milt Bernhart used to produce an annual luncheon in Los Angeles for ASMAC (the American Society of Motion Picture Arrangers and Composers), and he once invited me to present a short "dessert" program of my songs. I wrote "Sideman" for that occasion, and I was confident that the sentiments expressed in the lyric would be warmly appreciated by that crowd. An interviewer once asked me to speculate on what would be my favorite audience, and I told her it would be a gathering of retired dance band musicians. So this was the perfect opportunity, the perfect audience.

I got into the business at the very tail end of the big band era, so I never experienced the brutal schedules of bus rides and one-nighters and sleepless nights and days that constituted the life of yesterday's traveling sideman. I had a taste of it for several months in 1959 on the road with Kai Winding's band, and it was more laughs than complaining. No buses, but plenty of driving, and the occasional train.

When I compose lyrics I sometimes refer to my personal feelings when selecting the words that the singer is singing, but only rarely do I feel that the singer is "me," or that I am expressing my own thoughts. "Sideman" is an exception; it's me talking, despite the references to pressing my own pants, and doubling on flute.

I seriously take pleasure in being a sideman—the role of accompanist or ensemble player is a lot more fun than playing by myself, and it's far more enjoyable and much less excruciating than writing songs.

E-mail Conversation with Jack Berry, March 27–29, 2010

Berry:

I'm crazy about E-flat. On the guitar, it doesn't matter, but E-flat is more difficult to play on the piano. So what role does the ease of playing a key on a given instrument play?

Frishberg:

E-flat is less easy than what? The "ease of a key" will be different for different musical situations. Most American pop songs from the "classic" era are written in flat keys or "C-related" keys like G or F, because all brass and woodwind instruments are built in flat keys. String players, including guitar players(?), are less daunted by sharp keys, because the strings are normally tuned on tones in the sharp scale like E, A, G, D, etc., and that's where they shine.

Berry:

Are some tunes key indifferent and others key dependent?

Frishberg:

It depends on who's playing and on what instrument. Although here's something to consider: The "ease" of a key can also derive from the relative complexity of reading notation in that key signature. It's tough (for me) to read music in B because the key signature is either six sharps or seven flats (C-flat), and unless you're accustomed to seeing that and working with music in that key it's a pain in the ass to read. Everything looks unfamiliar

Generally speaking, jazz and dance band musicians are more involved with flat key signatures than they are with sharps, so they normally feel more comfortable in A-flat or D-flat than in E or A. Country musicians and folk musicians are more comfortable in sharp keys. They think in sharp keys because they're dealing with strings for the most part. Rock and hip-hop musicians are dealing with their own conventions and musical ethics, and they probably have their own preferences regarding key signatures and such. Classical players see it all, but I'm sure they are uncomfortable with awkward keys that are hard to read.

In other words, I would say there's nothing inherently difficult with certain keys—it's a matter of what you're accustomed to. Also, the more accidentals in the key signature, the more difficult it is to READ, and therefore may be experienced as "a difficult key." Regarding improvising in jazz, very few jazz players "think" in sharp keys, so they tend to shy away from keys like E, A, or B. For instance I can more easily grasp music spelled in flats—so I think of "Body and Soul" in D-flat rather than in C-sharp, even though the same pitches are involved.

Musicians play in all keys in the course of their careers. Those who work with singers, who are free from considerations of "hard" or "easy" keys, tend to be more adaptable and comfortable dealing with transposing in all key signatures. Although I must admit that if a singer asks me to fake "All the Things You Are" in A, I might just play it in A-flat or B-flat and won't bother to let them know. I mean, gimme a break.

Interesting question though.

Berry:

I'm hoping for a little bit of enlargement on my question: "Are some tunes key indifferent and others key dependent?"

Frishberg:

Pop songs each have a "standard key"—usually the key signature on the sheet music. Musicians who are building a repertoire learn songs in the standard keys, but it's not uncommon to encounter songs "on the job" that are to be played in a non-standard key.

I think songs will sound relatively the same when played in different keys, but certain keys will be appropriate, probably because of the range of the melody, and how it accommodates the range of the singer or the range of the instrument that's playing. Most singers find the highest (or lowest) pitch they'll need to sing, and then select a key that puts that note comfortably within their range. (Except for Nancy King, who sings in whatever key you're playing in—no problem).

Transposition of pop songs is a basic skill for professional dance band players. Players who are reading sometimes find that transposing might make certain written passages difficult, awkward, or even impossible, in which case they may grumble, "This is a hard key."

Berry:

I was also trying to get at something I've heard musicians say, that a given song sounds better in one key than another. Do you have any thoughts on that?

Frishberg:

Seems to me that ballads in the key of D-flat sound mellow on a grand piano, whereas on an upright piano I don't hear that difference. Must have something to do with sympathetic vibrations of wood and string elements. Also, any music in the key of D sounds brighter than the same music in the key of E-flat. And a D-minor triad out of context sounds more mournful than an E-minor triad out of context. This is pretty mysterious stuff, and if there's an acoustic explanation I'm not aware of it.

As a solo pianist, I often play standard songs in non-standard keys if they happen to lie better on the keyboard—for me.

Jazz Orthodoxy

I can't tell one current jazz piano player from another. They all sound pretty much the same to me. Everything is drenched in harmony. The harmonic ethic seems to be driving practically all jazz whether it's composed or improvised. Like most jazz instrumentalists, pianists seem intent on proclaiming their orthodoxy, so what you get is souped-up chords at every turn. Not one dominant seventh chord shall pass unaltered, and suspensions shall proceed unresolved, unless they're intended to be ironic. Fudge is great, but a total fudge diet is far too rich.

The scale exercises that Coltrane was fascinated with served him well because he developed a whole style out of it. But the kind of dumbed-down harmonic framework that resulted from his personal experimentation is not especially helpful if one is trying to communicate a range of expression through music.

What is often communicated instead is the player's stubborn determination to adhere to the personal peculiarities of somebody else's musical ethic, usually Miles, Bird, Coltrane, Bill Evans, Monk, and other icons. It's like speaking English with a thick Hungarian accent because you admire Béla Bartók's music.

The weakest element in jazz is the emphasis on improvisation—the long solos, the long procession of soloists. Listening to jazz players improvise is like hearing proficient musicians practicing from the same book of exercises. And that can get boring. Composed music is a much more effective way to grab the listener's attention and control it. (Playing dance music is a whole different ball game).

Sonny Rollins and Paul Desmond come to mind as examples of improvisers. Charlie Parker and Bud Powell are examples of innovative stylists. They are expert improvisers of course, as are many professional musicians, but that's not their strong suit. Bird and Powell have each created his own language, his own "vocabulary" as I like to think of it, and that is their message. On the other hand, Rollins and Desmond are more like narrators; they spin out coherent musical thoughts that connect with both our musical and our semantic receptors. To me, that makes for more interesting and engaging music.

Critics

After I'd been in New York for a few years I began to see my name mentioned in newspapers and magazines, as accompanist for singers and sideman with jazz groups. I think the first time that my piano playing was evaluated by a jazz critic was a comment in the *New Yorker*, referring to me as a "who's got the ball pianist," which I felt was pretty cold. But all in all, reviewers have been positive, and in many cases enthusiastically so.

One incident stands out as an example of horrible coverage by a jazz reviewer. During the early 1960s I played a two-week engagement in Canada with Buck Clayton's quintet along with saxist Buddy Tate, drummer Jackie Williams, and bassist Al Lucas. One night when I arrived for work my bandmates seemed nervous when they said hello to me. Buck said, "Did you see the review this morning?" I told him I knew nothing about a review. "Well, you don't want to see this story," said Buck. I found a copy of the local paper in the dressing room, and I was shocked to read what the critic had written about my piano playing. I forget the words, but it went something like:

"David Frishberg, the white pianist, should be ashamed of himself. He doesn't belong on the stage with these players. His piano contributions were pitiful and added nothing to the ensemble."

I was sitting in a chair, dazed and hurt. Buck Clayton said, "Don't pay any attention to this guy; he's vicious and crazy, and nobody takes him seriously. He rips musicians every week, and he's kind of famous for that."

A few nights later at the bar, a man tapped me on the shoulder and said (and I'm not making this up), "Mr. Frishberg, I write about jazz for the local paper. I certainly enjoy your playing; it's unique." I said, "Why don't you put that in the paper?" I was really upset and angry, but I didn't wait for his reply.

When I moved to Los Angeles and began to sing my songs in small local nightclubs, the critics were complimentary and encouraging. I got a call from Fat Tuesday's, a New York night club, to play there for a week with a trio.

This was my first time in New York since I'd left five years before, and here I was, featured as a singer (!), and singing my own songs. I got drummer Maurice Mark and bassist Rufus Reid, and we had a hurried rehearsal at the club on the afternoon of the opening. A bunch of my friends attended that night, and I was knocked out to see Al Cohn and Zoot Sims, with spouses, at a nearby table. What a night! My heart was leaping as we began the show.

I noticed immediately that the man and woman seated to my right at ringside were deep in conversation. As the show proceeded, they chattered on. I delivered my lyrics with difficulty because these folks were frowning and commenting as I sang. They rolled their eyes in exasperation when they heard a rhyme they didn't approve of. I was distracted by these two whispering hecklers throughout the entire set. Even though they stopped short of shouting nasty things at me, I felt heckled for sure.

At intermission I asked the manager, "What's with the couple in front? They didn't shut up for a second—thank God they're gone."

"Oh, that's the music critic. He writes for the paper."

Whoops.

Sure enough, a few days later I saw the jazz column in the popular local paper. The critic told of three jazz pianists who had each left New York and moved to Los Angeles: Ross Tompkins, Roger Kellaway, and Dave Frishberg. He noted that the first two had maintained their serious jazz careers even as they enjoyed high status Hollywood studio work, while (in so many words) Frishberg had caved in and sold out, and now writes funny songs that aren't as funny as he thinks they are.

This from a guy who jabbered all through my show. I was pissed off, and I held a grudge for many years. Not so much because of his fanciful allegations that I had somehow traded away my musical integrity, but because he distracted me and heckled me while I was trying to perform in front of an audience.

Wouldn't you know, a few years later, when I played at another New York club, he introduced himself, claiming that he admired my work. I was rude to him and told him I wasn't interested in discussing music with him.

Some critics in London were perplexed the first time I played and sang at the swanky nightclub Pizza on the Park, and a few were still scratching their heads years later when I had been engaged there for the fourth time. One reviewer said the audience "responded with puzzled applause," which I thought was a neat turn of phrase. Another was outraged that I had presented a song about baseball. He asked how I would feel if someone came to my country and sang about cricket? In my hotel room I composed a letter explaining that "Van Lingle Mungo" isn't about baseball, it's about names. But what the hell, I didn't send it. One mustn't fret about such matters.

Five

Too Long in L.A.

Too Long in L.A.

Waiting in the left-turn lane
Trying not to go insane
Squeezing on the steering wheel so tight
I can see my knuckles turning white
I've been missing every light in sight
And I've been driving all day
I've been living too long, too long
In L.A.

Should have gone Cahuenga Pass
Could have stopped and got some gas
Had I known this signal was so slow
I would have hung a left two lights ago
There's got to be a faster way I know
But I'll be late anyway
I've been living too long, too long in L.A.

Just got off the four oh five
Lucky to get off alive
People ought to learn to drive
Makes me want to call Rush Limbaugh

Longest light I've ever seen
Now the arrow turns to green
Driver in the SUV ahead
Decides to make a cell phone call instead
Now the arrow's changing back to red
I guess this isn't my day
I've been living too long, too long
Too long in L.A.

What's the story with this light?
Do I have to wait all night?
Trying not to get uptight
Where's the Xanax when you need it?

This expletive deleted car
Can take me only just so far
And then I'm going to make that change of pace
And find myself a primo parking place
Then I'll be saying "So long, so long
I'm on my way"
'Cause I've been living too long too long, too long in L.A.

Words and music by Dave Frishberg
©1995 Swiftwater Music

Frishberg vs. the Music Business

If it's arguable that anyone can make music, it seems clear that anyone can publish it. I've met a few people in the music publishing game who have good taste in music, but they seemed to regard that as a private matter that needn't get in the way of business. Until I began dealing with David Rosner in the late 1960s, the publishers I did business with in New York might just as well have been selling auto parts or fur coats for all the insight they had into their products or their inventories. Also, many of them were primarily active as writers or producers, and that group was notorious for being neglectful of their "publishing sideline." They merely collected copyrights.

Even big-name publishers in lavish offices were often rude, insulting, and not averse to swindling a young hopeful songwriter. They would listen distractedly to a song from behind a desk, sometimes interrupted by phone calls, then whip out a blank contract and say, "Lemme run with this. Sign right here." There was never a discussion of an advance, and I didn't even know that legitimate publishers routinely offered advance money in exchange for ownership of a copyright. I actually fell for this a few times, and gave away songs for nothing. I was flattered that a real "publisher" liked my song, and I believed that by signing a contract at this guy's desk, I had actually placed my song "on the market." Boy, was I mistaken.

Of course, where I had really placed the song was in the publisher's file cabinet. Having invested zero in the song, he would promptly forget about it, and file it away with hundreds of titles in his catalog. Every dollar that the song might earn for the rest of my life would pass through this guy's office first, and he then was supposed to split it with me. There was no attempt to promote or show the song. Since it was typically through my own efforts, sometimes years later, that a song of mine got heard and recorded and sold on the market, I would chuckle ruefully when a check for $35 from an unfamiliar publisher would come in the mail, and I'd remember that somewhere, some stranger from long ago named Artie was keeping $35 for himself. If you've got a ton of copyrights in your file cabinet, you could succeed handsomely as a "music publisher" on your cut of the proceeds, and all this without lifting a finger to market the songs. And if you decide not to honor the contract, you could keep *all* the proceeds, and the writer would never know unless he took costly measures to find out.

In those days, especially after I moved to Los Angeles, I mistrusted publishers and other show-business dealmakers in general. I was convinced that they were in the business essentially to fleece the writers, performers, artists, and other "talent."

I think the music publishing business took this turn after printed music began to go out of fashion, and radio stations began to play songs written by folk musicians, kids, and other do-it-yourself composers. The function of "publisher" was transformed gradually into the role of an agent, or performance plugger, or some other vaguely defined benefactor, who through their "connections" could make radio play and hence record sales possible for the new population of "civilian" songwriters and troubadours. A lot of young people were getting lucky, and the "publishing," whatever that meant, was worth 50 percent of the proceeds of each mammoth stroke of good fortune. It didn't take long for the songwriters, me included, to figure out that the smart thing to do is "publish" your own material. That way, when you get lucky, you collect 100 percent.

It was shortly after I moved to Portland in 1986 that I finally stopped holding on stubbornly but ineffectively as owner/administrator of my company Swiftwater Music, which I had been trying to operate since its inception in Los Angeles in 1974. I couldn't keep up with the paperwork, nor did I have the slightest inkling of how to find songwriting money and collect it.

David Rosner is the one who demonstrated to me how a professional music publisher works to activate copyrights, derives income from them, and checks the numbers, and he did it with my own songs. He even retrieved from Frank Music some songs that I had given away to them back in the early New York days. One of them was "Peel Me a Grape," which had been sitting idle in a file cabinet for twenty-five years. I wouldn't have dared to ask them for the song back, but Rosner persistently pleaded my case that they had kept the song under wraps along with a handful of others for a quarter century. My total income from all the songs during Frank's administration had been less than $500. Rosner twisted the arm of Frank Music's attorney John Eastman, until Eastman gave the songs back, grumbling, "These aren't exactly our big moneymakers."

Bob Dorough and I took our song "I'm Hip" to several publishers during the early 1960s. They each kept a copy of the song, but as far as I know, there were no contracts signed or agreements made, and none of the publishers took any action with the song. About ten years later, Bob and I had occasion to trace the copyright history of "I'm Hip" when we discovered that royalties from a Blossom Dearie recording were being paid to the wrong publisher. We were certain that we owned the song jointly with our own publishing companies, but surprise! Here was evidence that three other publishers had registered "I'm Hip" with ASCAP back in the early '60s, and one other publisher had registered it with BMI as well as with European licensing agencies. We recognized the names involved and got it straightened out with a few phone calls. But it was discouraging and depressing to find out that people we had considered friends and allies were so casual about claiming ownership of our song.

During the 1980s in L.A., I got a small sum of money from a Dutch company called Three Peters. The accompanying letter referred to a sub-publishing agreement made a year earlier with Swiftwater Music, my company. David Rosner runs Swiftwater Music with an eagle eye, and he was mystified. About a dozen titles were involved. including a couple that belonged to third-party publishers, and Rosner had certainly not made such a deal. We found through investigation that a well-known San Francisco attorney whom I had met briefly once at the Washington Square Bar and Grill, did business with Three Peters while traveling in the Netherlands, claimed to be authorized to make European agreements on behalf of Swiftwater Music, and was given a cash advance. I called the guy in San Francisco and asked him how much Three Peters paid him, and how he convinced them that he represented Swiftwater. He laughed, invited me to sue him, and told me to go fuck myself. I still hear references made to this gentleman, who nowadays is a prominent defense lawyer in Bay Area drug cases.

David Rosner entered my life back in New York in the late 1960s, when I was hustling my songs around to different publishers. Our mutual friend Margo Guryan (who subsequently married David) had brought me to Rosner's office at April Music to show him my new song "Oklahoma Toad." I was trying earnestly at that time to write "contemporary," and David and Margo took me and my writing very seriously. I was under the spell of the Four B's—Beatles, Beach Boys, Bacharach, and the Brazilians—and David and Margo shared my enthusiasm.

I was continuing to write songs for other people to sing, Rosner was publishing them, and in the process of making demos I became interested in performing the songs myself, because after all, I knew how they were supposed to go. I wrote a handful of what I considered "country western" songs, a few baleful ballads, and a few novelty songs that bordered on the surrealistic.

About a year later, David and Margo produced my first album, all original songs, aimed at the youthful market. The LP, titled *Oklahoma Toad*, came out in 1970 on the CTI label. One of the songs, "Van Lingle Mungo," got some airplay and spontaneous publicity in the sports pages nationwide.

Not Just a Sideman

So you ask how I became known as a singer and songwriter rather than a sideman.

During the '70s, my friend drummer Bill Goodwin invited me to the Poconos to record songs that I had written and had been singing and playing in small clubs in Los Angeles. Bill was president and head of production for a small record company called Omni Sound and a strong believer in my songs, singing, and playing, having heard me on the unsuccessful *Oklahoma Toad*. I thought this a good opportunity. I recorded two albums for Omni Sound, both of which were recorded at Mountain Sound by engineer Chris Fichera. Besides producing both recordings, Bill played drums and swept up the studio afterward. Steve Gilmore played bass.

The first recording, which took several days, was *The Dave Frishberg Songbook, Vol. 1*, which was released in 1981 and nominated in 1982 for a Grammy for Best Jazz Vocal Performance—Male. The second recording, *The Dave Frishberg Songbook, Vol. 2*, was nominated for a Grammy in 1983 in the same category. Bill tells me these albums were the most successful recordings of Omni Sound and reminds me how, before the second album was nominated for a Grammy, I held it up for the audience to see while a guest on Johnny Carson's *Tonight Show*.

So I guess this is how I became better known as a Singer and Songwriter.

Omni Sound folded and I was able to acquire the masters for those recordings. Thereafter, I produced for Fantasy Records *Live at Vine Street*, which was recorded live at the Vine Street Bar and Grill in Hollywood, California, and nominated for another Grammy in 1985. I also produced for Fantasy *Can't Take You Nowhere*, recorded live at the Great American Music Hall in San Francisco, which was nominated for another Grammy in 1987. Both these nominations were for Best Jazz Vocal Performance—Male.

Concord Records reissued the two Omni Sound Records as *Classics*.

The Funny Side

During the winter and spring of 1971 I was playing piano onstage for a play at the Vivian Beaumont Theater at the Lincoln Center for the Performing Arts in New York. The play was *Scenes from American Life* by A. R. Gurney Jr. I think it may have been his first produced play. The cast included James Broderick, Christopher Walken, and Priscilla Pointer, and it was directed by Dan Sullivan. (I think it was his first New York directing job). The play observed the life of a Buffalo, New York, society family through four decades, and the scenes took place in the past, present, and future, not in chronological order. My function was to play transitions to establish the time frame for each scene and to play musical cues and underscoring, and accompany the occasional dancing or singing moments. The author specified every song that should be played, including pop songs, hymns, Bach chorales, folk songs, collegiate rally music, and operatic quotes. Example: (A FATHER and SON settle into two chairs, placed to indicate a sailboat. The piano plays a wry arrangement of "SAILING, SAILING." The FATHER pantomimes working the tiller, adjusting the mainsheet. The SON looks off dreamily.) There were thirty-six cues specified, and I played a twelve-minute "overture" before the actors entered.

I was living apart from Stella now, subletting a grim third-floor walk-up, a rear apartment in an ancient brownstone on West End and 91st Street. I was getting restless in New York, work was getting scarcer, and the play was ending its run, as was my marriage. I had the feeling that if something came up, I'd be ready to leave New York.

I got a phone call from Sam Denoff and Bill Persky, my old pals at WNEW. They were now rich and famous in L.A. with their hit series *The Dick Van Dyke Show*. They were producing a new series for NBC called *The Funny Side*, a weekly variety show, and they had heard songs from my LP *Oklahoma Toad*, and they wondered if I'd be interested in writing comedy songs for the show. "Of course," I said.

They flew me to Los Angeles, and I met with Sam and Bill, arrangers Jack Elliott and Allyn Ferguson, and Ray Charles (of the Ray Charles Singers). I played and sang some of my stuff for them, and they went for it. I was hired. I would be writing original songs for each show. It was all humor-oriented, and I would join their staff of eminent comedy writers and operate out of their office at NBC in Burbank. There was no talk of money, no contract, no agreement. "Just move out here," Bill Persky told me, "and get settled in. We'll start in about three months. By the time we get going, we'll have an agreement with you, and we'll make a deal."

~

I arrived in Los Angeles in early July of 1971 and moved into my cousin Ruth Greenberg's vacant apartment in Westwood. I had a little office at NBC with a typewriter and a spinet. The team of comedy writers occupied the offices down the hall. All day these guys were "on," jabbering and laughing and trying to break each other up. On the first day, I drove back to my apartment and began writing there, where there was peace and quiet. I composed on my Wurlitzer electric piano, which I had shipped from New York. Each week I wrote one of these comedic production numbers on the assigned topic—a total of nine. The show was canceled before number nine aired.

Today, as I listen to my songs as they sounded on the air, taped with a microphone in front of the TV speaker, I'm struck by the middle-class white-bread tone of the whole thing. The sexism is especially remarkable.

Each week the show dealt with the "funny side" of a certain area of life. The cast of ten were five heavily "typical" couples as follows:

YUPPIE COUPLE—Dick Claire and Jenna McMahon
BLACK COUPLE—John Amos and Teresa Graves
OCTOGENARIAN COUPLE—Burt Mustin and Queenie Smith
BLUE-COLLAR COUPLE—Warren Berlinger and Pat Finley
TEENAGE COUPLE—Michael Lembeck and Cindy Williams

The host was Gene Kelly.

The full cast ensemble production numbers were prerecorded and then lip-synched before the live audience. Otherwise everything was live. All the songs were elaborately blocked and choreographed. This added to the frustration and impatience of the actors, who had an hour's worth of sketches to learn each week, and who were not primarily singers or dancers. For "The Funny Side of Newspapers," Warren Berlinger sang "The Sports Page" live on camera, complete with tricky soft-shoe moves and much business with lunch pail and hard hat. He got so upset that he kicked his hat across the stage, and they had to tape the number three or four times until he got it right. He was really teed off. They had him doing high kicks while singing the last chorus.

The Sports Page

I

My friendly TV anchorman says watch the Middle East
The price of oil is going out of sight.
Only yesterday he said the price would never be increased,
And that's the opposite of what he said last night.

Now it's getting so tough to understand this stuff
I don't really want to bother anymore.
If I want to understand the news that I read today
I gotta forget the news I read the day before.

But then I turn to the sports page
And I find out that the Lakers didn't make it.
There's no way I know they can fake it.
They can't say they win if they lose.

It's right there on the sports page.
There's no way I know to deny it.
They win, they lose, or they tie it.
They can't cover it up in the news.

II
Now generals and congressmen and other shifty guys
They all got little tricks they like to pull,
And the scratchy stuff I feel that's being pulled around my eyes
I'm beginning to identify as wool.

On today's front page some joker half my age
Is telling what he knows about the war.
By the time I read his version of what I'm supposed to know
I know even less than what I knew before

But then I turn to the sports page
And I read where Reggie Jackson made an error.
Now how can they report that any fairer?
(The sun must have got in his eyes.)

It's right there on the sports page;
It's just the simple facts that I am finding,
And not another axe somebody's grinding.
They can't change the score by printing lies.

III

I remember back one season when the Mets were riding high,
The astronauts were landing on the moon.
I watched it on the TV, and I looked up at the sky,
And then I started laughing like a loon.

It could all be a fake like a movie they could make,
And we'd all believe they're really out in space.
And the Russians could be busy making phony movies too,
And we'd never know who really won the race.

Then I turned to the sports page,
And the Mets had blown it in the thirteenth inning.
The papers can't make losing look like winning.
(I think the Phillies took it five to four.)

There it was on the sports page,
The only page that takes a firm position.
Sort of like an honest politician,
The kind you hardly find anymore
In fact, let's face it:
The sports page is the only place to go
When a fella wants to know the score.

Words and music by Dave Frishberg for the NBC series *The Funny Side*
© 1971 Swiftwater Music/Funny Side Music (renewed)

Ferguson and Elliott wrote very good arrangements, and the orchestra
was populated by the cream of L.A. studio cats. I knew a few members

of the orchestra from New York days. Now, as I listen to "Save Us from Sunday," the first song I wrote for the series, I remember the terror that gripped me during the prerecording as I sat in the booth and heard Gene Kelly stumble again and again over his vocal entrance. He complained that he couldn't feel the timing of it and asked conductor Jack Elliott if the beginning of the song could somehow be simplified. Elliott consulted with me, and I told him that if he could think of anything simpler than an eighth rest and a dotted quarter he could be my guest. I said, "I thought this guy was musical." Elliott said, "He is. From the ankles down."

The Deal

So what happened with "the deal" that finally was agreed upon? I anticipated around $1,000 per show. Persky introduced me to George Shapiro, the lawyer who was negotiating all the contracts for *The Funny Side*. Shapiro and I sat down together in his office at NBC, and he began to talk:

"I haven't heard your stuff, but I hear you do good work. Look, nobody knows who you are, you don't have an agent representing you, and this is your first job in television. The agreement will be for the first season of *The Funny Side*. When the show is renewed for another season, we'll negotiate again—you should get an agent, by the way—and the money will be better. Right now at this stage, everybody on the team is working for practically nothing, so I hope you'll understand why the numbers seem a little low. Once your name gets around town, and people see your credits on TV, you'll do better and things will be different."

"So your job will be to write original words and music as needed for each weekly episode. NBC will own all the rights to everything you contribute. Songs are due every Monday morning at cast read-through. Jack Elliott and Allyn Ferguson will orchestrate, and you will be paid a weekly salary of $292, from which taxes will be withheld."

Shapiro saw the distressed reaction on my face. "Look," he told me, "I haven't heard your stuff, but Persky and Denoff really want you on this show. To be honest with you, we have other alternatives." I sat there stunned. I was working at NBC, writing for a weekly comedy series; I'd already contributed two songs; and the girl who answered the phone was earning more than I was. I was doing a lot better back at the Vivian Beaumont Theater. There was nothing to say.

I strolled back into Persky's office, and he and Denoff were standing at the window looking out at the NBC parking lot. Bill said, "Hey Davey, look at this! They're delivering my new Bentley." It was perfect, and I had to laugh.

The Ballad of Ralph Nader

The Ballad of Ralph Nader

I

When Ralph Nader was a boy his daddy brought him home a toy
And the dang thing fell apart that very day.
Ralphie hollered long and loud, then he calmed down and he vowed
He would get the crooks who cheated him that way.

Now they can't tempt him, they can't scare him,
They can't bribe him heaven knows
'Cause a million bucks he'd gladly sacrifice.
His life is dedicated to protecting us from those
Who try to sell us shoddy merchandise.

Go on and ride, Ralph Nader, ride
Straight ahead with confidence and pride.
All across our mighty nation folks are filled with admiration
And we're proud we got Ralph Nader on our side.

II
Some supermarket hustlers, just like old-time cattle rustlers
Were tryin' to pull a fast one with their meat.
But oblivious to danger, that Ivy League lone ranger said,
"Now hold it boys, this meat ain't fit to eat!"
Then Ralph Nader formed a posse
And they ran them rustlers down,
And showed all the world about their dirty game.

Now the common folks all love him
And the crooks are frightened of him.
Even corporations tremble at his name.

Go on and ride, Ralph Nader, ride
Straight ahead with confidence and pride.
All across our mighty nation folks are filled with admiration
and we're proud we got Ralph Nader on our side.

III
Ralph Nader took the wheel of his brand-new automobile
And everything stopped running but the clock.
He said, "This engine's just a joke,
and I think the brakes are broke.
It ain't safe to drive this thing around the block!"

He walked straight into the factory,
Called the biggest boss aside,
Told him, "Better straighten out or you'll be sunk

'Cause the people will awaken
when I show them what you're makin'
Ain't nothin' but a brand-new piece of junk."

Go on and ride, Ralph Nader, ride
Straight ahead with confidence and pride
All across our mighty nation folks are filled with admiration
And we're proud we got Ralph Nader on our side.

Words and music by Dave Frishberg for the NBC series *The Funny Side*
© 1971 Swiftwater Music/Funny Side Music

The Ralph Nader song was featured on "The Funny Side of Politics." The two teenagers sang it near the end of the show, and then the audience joined in with the entire cast for the big finale. The song really worked; the audience loved it, as did the cast. But *The Funny Side*, which was not very funny at all, was discontinued by NBC after eight episodes.

About thirty years later Nader was running for president. I was on his side, so I rewrote the lyric and offered the song to the manager of the Nader campaign in Portland, Oregon:

Now in times of boom and bust, we need a leader we can trust
So our way of life don't slide on down the drain.
Ralph Nader knows the score, he's got ideas and what is more
He possesses both a conscience and a brain.

He's no sleazy politician, 'cause this man is not for sale
And he's not about to make no shady deal.
He really gets intense in the cause of common sense
So the people know Ralph Nader is for real.

Go on and ride, Ralph Nader, ride.
We're backing you with confidence and pride.
Senior citizens, consumers, teenage kids and baby boomers
We are proud, we are proud
We are proud we got Ralph Nader on our side.

Nader's Portland campaign manager was not impressed. "Jazz it up a little," he suggested, and I assured him I would. We never spoke after that.

By this time, I was playing regularly in local nightclubs and having a ball. I had a neat little one-bedroom apartment in the Lake Hollywood neighborhood near the top of Barham Boulevard. I was working regularly in local nightclubs with jazz groups and singers. I was writing and producing radio commercials for a jingle outfit.

A bunch of my New York musician friends had moved to Los Angeles with *The Tonight Show Starring Johnny Carson* and *The Merv Griffin Show*, and they hung out at Donte's, the jazz club in North Hollywood. I became a frequent sideman there, playing with a wide variety of headliners. I lived nearby, so I was in Donte's practically every night whether I was working there or not. I began to get calls for studio work, including occasional subbing in Doc Severinsen's *Tonight Show* band, and playing on sound tracks for jingles, TV shows, and movies. After those few months writing special material songs under pressure, I had some momentum going. When Bob Dorough called from New York and invited me to contribute songs for the *Schoolhouse Rock* TV series, I was ready. I was busy, and making fairly good money, but I didn't like living in L.A. From my very first day there, I felt it was a malignant environment, and I knew I would get out of there someday. "Someday" turned out to be fifteen years later.

2 Percent Panic

My first experience in a recording studio was in 1947 when my brother Mort was home on leave from the navy and the two of us performed at Schmitt Music in Minneapolis. The recordings were made direct to disc, of course, the stylus inscribing the sounds onto acetate discs revolving at 78 rpm. You walked away with acetate platters so soft that they could withstand only a few playings before they deteriorated into near uselessness. We played the discs carefully and not very often.

I was fourteen and very wrapped up in learning the blues on the piano, and I displayed my repertoire of boogie-woogie pieces I had copied from records. I recorded a couple of titles by Pete Johnson, including my favorite—"KC on My Mind"; also "Detroit Rocks," by Montana Taylor; "Honky Tonk Train," by Meade Lux Lewis; and an original blues of my own devising called "Heavy Hearted Blues." "Heavy-Handed Blues" would be more like it. Mort joined me for "Roll 'Em Pete" with a vocal that sounds very much like Joe Turner on the famous record.

Eventually I made tapes of these recordings, so the contents would be protected from deterioration, relatively speaking. My playing sounds unrefined but confident and energetic. Fifty years later I sent a cassette to Mort in L.A., and I am told he listened again and again to "Roll 'Em Pete." My first real professional record date was in New York in the spring of 1958. I had recently quit my day job at RCA Victor and was playing piano full-time. Much of my work was rehearsing with singers. I was accompanying occasionally in Leonard (Zeke) Frank's vocal studio in Carnegie Hall. Zeke was a voice teacher with an interesting and talented bunch of clients, among them Barbara Cook, Carmen McRae, and Stella Graham (Giammasi), who subsequently became my wife. Zeke would produce demo recordings for his stable of singers, sometimes marketing them on his Stardust label. His musical director was often Mat Mathews, a wild jazz accordionist from the Netherlands who was a fast and clever arranger. Mat heard me play one day up at Zeke's studio, and told Zeke that he should use me on some recordings.

A week later I got a phone call from Mat. "Zeke's got a record date for you tomorrow with one of his chickies, ten in the morning. Can you make it?" Naturally I was thrilled to be asked, but I was also a little scared, because this meant I would be tested and my reading skills would be on display. "Don't worry about it," Mat said. "You can play this shit. Be at Bell Sound ten tomorrow morning. It's a good band."

Good band was right. The next morning I walked in and there was Clark Terry, trumpet; J. J. Johnson, trombone; Jerome Richardson and Big Nick Nicholas on sax; Everett Barksdale on guitar; Wendell Marshall, bass; and Osie Johnson, drums. Mat was running the date from the booth. This was the "A-team" of New York session players. I didn't know these men except by reputation of course. We recorded two songs: "Rockin' Flapper," an original by the singer's manager, and the well-known "Prisoner of Love."

I had no problem with either piece of music. I carefully read and played every note in every measure, intent on not making a mistake—after all, wasn't that my job? The piano part for "Prisoner of Love" was page after page of a simple triplet figure. "Aaaah—lone from night to night Yooooool . . . find me . . ." There the triplets began and persisted all the way to the end. We made a complete take and I kept my eyes glued to the music, executing each triplet exactly as it was written. When we finished, after the customary silence, the rhythm section players were in hysterics. Osie Johnson yelled, "You read every goddamn triplet! You don't have to do that! Just play!" After the laughter died down, Osie said, "You know what? It felt good." Which I never forgot. That was the only time that I ever played with Osie Johnson. His words that morning meant a lot to me.

When I moved to L.A. I had better connections in the recording world, and I did a lot more studio work there than I did in New York. In 1980 I played piano on some film dates for a talented young composer named Miles Goodman who was just starting out in the business. He called me one day and said, "I'm scoring a film about the Harlem Globetrotters, and I'm going to use their theme song 'Sweet Georgia Brown.' You know that song?" I told him I sure did. He said, "I'll write it to feature piano—rinky-tink style. What key do you like to play it in?" I told him that the original key is A-flat and that would be fine with me. "Okay," Miles said, "A-flat it is."

When I got to the studio, there was a good-size string section assembled, with winds and brass, harp, and three percussionists. As usual, the parts were designated by numbers, not by titles. We recorded M-10, M-11, and M-12. I looked at the next cue, M-13, and my heart sank when I saw the key signature—seven flats. What was going on here? The piano part was black with notes. Then I saw that the melody began on an A-flat seventh chord, and I realized what had happened. This was "Sweet Georgia Brown," and Goodman, in all innocence, had assumed that my choice of A-flat meant that I wanted to begin the song with an A-flat seventh chord, which of course placed the song in the key of C-flat.

Already the shouts and groans had begun in the string section. "What are you doing to us? Why are we playing in this key?" I began to fumble around with my piano part, and the concertmaster stood up and spoke very loudly to Goodman, who was standing with a baton, ready to start the orchestra. "Miles, this is 'Sweet Georgia Brown,' for Chrissake! Why are we reading it in seven flats? This is bullshit!"

Miles pointed to me and said, "That's where Dave wanted it." I stood up then and began to defend myself, but before I could say a word, guitarist Tommy Tedesco shouted, "Hey Frishberg, I don't play in seven flats for scale!" and the whole orchestra broke up.

Miles quickly fixed it. He told everybody to lay out and told me to play the cue alone in my key of choice with a click track, which I did, with heart pounding. "We'll add the orchestra tomorrow," Miles announced, and everyone took a break. The next day, Miles told me that the solo piano worked fine, and he decided to leave it alone.

The prospect of performing "Sweet Georgia Brown" in C-flat in rinky-tink style—accompanied by an angry orchestra while the tape was running and the clock was ticking—had reduced me to jelly. I was always a little uneasy in anticipation of a recording date, because I knew there would someday be something I couldn't execute, and I would be exposed and labeled as "not first call" or, worse, "don't call him." There was a widely quoted formula that summed up the routine of the studio musician's life: "98 percent boredom and 2 percent panic."

I sailed along, got lucky, and did okay. Sometimes there would be another keyboard player there to switch parts with. Sometimes the arranger or the composer would say, "Piano, don't fight that figure. Just play something appropriate." But once in a while, precision was required, and I had to deliver a difficult exposed passage again and again while repeated takes were necessary because of a problem some-where else in the ensemble. I kept thinking, "Will I be the one to foul it up next time?" And when an acceptable take had been completed, I sat with pounding heart and sweating scalp, thanking the Lord that I'd never have to live that musical moment again.

As I mentioned, I had good connections and many pals who worked in the studios, and after a couple of years I got a call to play on some *Charlie's Angels* sound tracks. Television dates like this were sought after, especially the heavily syndicated ones like *Charlie's Angels*, because there could be decades of substantial residual payments. This was the kind of jackpot account that studio musicians aimed for; they built their retirement plans on gigs like these.

This kind of work was difficult for me to deal with because it consisted mainly of quick and accurate sight-reading, without a lot of personal interpretation. In other words, they wanted to hear the part, not Dave Frishberg playing the part. The music, designed to underscore action and enhance mood or motion, was recorded in separate segments called cues. Sometimes my part would be the featured melodic element in the cue, but most of the time I had no idea how my part might be fitting into the ensemble. To make the moment more intimidating, the part was likely to be written for an electronic keyboard I had never seen before, that I could barely operate unless someone programmed it for me. I would get to the date an hour early so I could learn how to turn the synthesizer on and to use some basic controls. Then the date would start, and I'd be praying before every take that my part wasn't crucial.

For the past four years I'd been trying to steer myself into the recording studios, and I felt I had made it. I couldn't help wondering: Do I really enjoy this? After several sessions, I respectfully requested that the contractor not call me for that type of work.

The Song of God

The most bizarre recording session I was ever associated with took place in Los Angeles in 1978. The call came one night from a man who was a complete stranger to me. He spoke with a Latin accent and he was shouting into the phone, "MISTER Frishberg! Are you SLEEPING? Why are you sleeping, the night is YOUNG!"

"Who is this?" I said.

"I am GOD," the man answered, "but you can call me Ricky, or

Rick, but I don't care what you call me, because all I care about is your PIANO!" The guy sounded like a lunatic, but the recording date as he described it seemed legitimate, and would pay union scale. "And a lot of your FRIENDS will be there!" the man snarled. "I don't know you, MISTER Frishberg. I really wanted Jimmy Rowles, but Jimmy Rowles couldn't MAKE IT, and he gave me your name and that's good enough for me. Steve Huffsteter is the leader and he will call you with the details." Huffsteter called the next day and confirmed. "Ricky is a nutcase," Steve explained, "but the date is for real."

The date took place late at night at T & R Studio in Hollywood on a giant soundstage that was used for big orchestras. I was surprised to find over a dozen musicians gathered there, including some big studio names: Shelly Manne, Chuck Domanico, Gary Foster, and other luminaries. Nobody knew what was happening. Steve Huffsteter and the other horn players were sitting in front of empty music stands. Clare Fischer was the other keyboard player, and he was preparing a giant synthesizer. There was a female singer, and she had no idea what to expect. Bill Hood was warming up his baritone sax, and he told me, "Wait 'til Ricky gets here. Anything's liable to happen."

Ricky burst in, nearly incoherent with excitement. He was a small man with a severe limp, crazed eyes, and a permanent snarl. "I AM HERE AND I AM GOD!" Ricky announced. Then he launched into a rambling screaming speech: "I called you because you men—AND WOMEN—WHATEVER—you have what I don't have myself! TALENT! I have no voice, I cannot sing! I cannot play an instrument, I cannot write music down, I can't even bang on a FUCKING DRUM!"

Shelly Manne piped up quietly, "No argument here, Ricky."

Ricky sailed on: "Now tonight—TONIGHT! I will be the artist. I will be the creator. It will be MY music. And you are MY VOICE.

THE VOICE OF GOD! and the music will come through you, because each of you has been INDIVIDUALLY SELECTED! BY GOD!"

Somebody called out, "So what are we playing? Some standard songs or what? Where's the music?"

Ricky answered, "I don't want STANDARD SONGS! There is no music. You don't NEED music. The music is you. You are my fingers, you are my brain—YOU ARE MY SONG! A NEW SONG! THE SONG OF GOD!"

Shelly Manne hollered, "What kind of mood did you have in mind?"

"MOOD? I'LL SHOW YOU WHAT MOOD!" And Ricky dumped a small mountain of cocaine on the desk in front of him.

So presently the musicians assembled at their instruments, and Clare Fischer took over instantly and naturally, and he began to put together the framework for a totally improvised piece. Clare was one of the most brilliant musicians in the business, and this kind of musical game was his cup of tea. Right off the top of his head, he began to invent a plan for the improvisation, and assigned metric, melodic, featured, and supporting roles. The unfortunate singer was panic-stricken, but somehow Clare showed her how and where she could fit in. Shelly Manne made some helpful suggestions, and everyone else, including me, kept quiet. There was no rehearsal as such.

Then we began to play: I don't remember the exact instrumentation, but it was something like two fully equipped percussionists, four brass, three reeds, two guitars, piano, synthesizer, two bass players, a violinist, and a singer. There were no parts, no notes, no words, no musical directions of any kind.

It seemed to roll along smoothly, and with Clare's gestures and musical cues, there was an actual development to a climax and a cooling down to the coda. I have no recollection of what the thing sounded like, but I remember that it was about five minutes long, and my main concern was to muffle my explosions of laughter so as not to ruin the track. Everybody was so professional, so sensitive, and so cooperative in the midst of this clearly preposterous situation that I couldn't help thinking, "Huffsteter called the right guys."

We listened to what we had played, and everybody had a good laugh. Ricky was not laughing with us, because he was ecstatic in the control booth. "I love it! THE SONG OF GOD!" he shouted. "That's the name of it, and it belongs to me, because I am God." Then he drifted off into meandering speculations about copyright and publishing, while the musicians packed up in the studio and everyone said good night. I asked the engineer to be sure to make a dub of the session for me, and he said he didn't have time right now, but he'd make a copy for me.

We subsequently got paid over the counter at the union with payroll checks through a payroll service, with deductions and all, as if this madness had been financed by an actual Hollywood production company, which was probably true. I tried to imagine the brain-shattering business lunch during which the budget for this project might have been discussed. My big disappointment about the whole job was that I never got a tape of the performance, as promised. I called Steve Huffsteter several times, questioning him about Ricky's project, but Steve never heard of it ever again, and he didn't have a tape either. I have a feeling that there is a tape somewhere.

I never saw Ricky again, but a few months later I did get some answering machine messages from him, shouting that he was GOD, which I recorded for posterity. Several years passed, and then Bill Hood sent me a newspaper clipping that listed a dozen bizarre and colorful name changes recently recorded in California courts. Among them was one Enrique S—of Marin County, who had legally changed his name to Universal Perpetual God. "You know who this is," Bill had written in the margin.

Yes, I Saw UFOs

In the late 1970s I played a few summer weekend gigs at Pasquale's in Malibu with bassist Pat Senatore and drummer Roy McCurdy. I was single in L.A. at the time and making the most of it. After work one night I got gabbing with some people at the bar, and they invited me to join them at their house on the beach. I thought that was a splendid idea. I drove up the coast a few miles and found the place. The people were a congenial bunch, tan and wealthy, smoking cigarettes and reefers, sipping scotch and sniffing cocaine. They were all strangers to me, but I did recognize a young woman named Barra, whom I had met several times at Donte's. I sat down and somebody handed me a pipe and said, "Care for some of this?"

"Sure, thanks," was my reply, and I took a healthy poke. "That's pretty strange-tasting pot," I said, and took another poke . . . "That's not pot," the guy said and started to laugh. I handed the pipe back to him and said, "Oh really? What is it?"

"Angel dust. I thought you knew that. Haven't you done that?"

"No, I'm afraid I've never done that," I said, and tried to stand up. My legs were jelly and I flopped back into my seat. "Look," I told him, "I don't think I'm enjoying this. This is elephant tranquilizer. This is not what I had in mind. This is not a good feeling."

"You'll be okay," said my new friend, lighting up and puffing. "Just roll with it."

"I'll roll all right." I staggered to my feet and headed for the deck that overlooked the beach. "I need some air," I said. "If I pass out, please take care of me."

"Don't worry about it."

Barra was out on the deck by herself. "What hit you?" she said. "Are you okay?"

I told her, "They're doing angel dust. I didn't know."

"Oh yeah, that's powerful stuff. They tranquilize elephants with that."

"To say the least."

My head was spinning. I took some deep breaths, hung on to the railing, and calmed down. We stared out at the sea, didn't say much for a couple of minutes. Then I looked up. The sky was suddenly alive with tiny lights, hundreds of lights splayed out all the way to the horizon and past, stretching from here to there, near to far. I asked Barra, "Are you seeing this?" She said she saw it. I said, "Have you ever seen anything like this?" Barra answered, "Never," and as she spoke, the entire sky-wide display changed in an instant; the lights rearranged themselves across the heavens, nearby lights leaping all the way back into the horizon and distant lights zooming up to the forefront. The entire repositioning took place in the blink of an eye. Then it happened again, all the lights grabbing new positions in the sky, then again.

"Barra, are you seeing this?" Barra nodded. "I sure am."

I said, "Things don't move that way. It's physically impossible. Am I hallucinating with this stuff?"

Barra said, "I didn't smoke any of that, and I'm seeing it."

Then the lights were gone, the show was over. I checked my watch, and said, "Give me your telephone number. I'll call you tomorrow when all this is over, and we'll compare notes on what we just witnessed." We joined the party back inside and told them about the light show, but the other guests hadn't noticed anything, and they were finding it difficult to concentrate on what we were saying. They just stared at us and laughed as if we were sharing a joke. I was finding it hard to concentrate myself. I don't remember driving home that night, but obviously I did, and the next day I called Barra. It all checked out; she had seen the same thing.

I called the UFO sighting station at Point Mugu naval observatory not far from Malibu, and I told them I had seen phenomenal things the previous night about 1:30 a.m. over the ocean. The navy guy said, "Yes. We've got other phone calls about what you're describing.

"Well, what was it?"

"We don't know, sir."

"Did you see it too?"

"I'm not allowed to discuss that, sir."

So that's the story. I saw UFOs over the ocean at Malibu. I'm not crazy, I can back it up. It was over twenty years later that I ran into Barra in a nightclub in L.A. "Did we see it?" I asked. Barra replied emphatically, "We did. We saw it."

So I saw UFOs. Who is going to believe my story? Okay, so I was under the influence of a chemical designed to sedate circus animals, but that's irrelevant and purely coincidental. I mean, ask Barra.

Johnny Mercer

I knew Johnny Mercer's daughter Amanda long before I ever met Mercer, because Mandy was married to my friend Bob Corwin, who was then the solo intermission pianist at Eddie Condon's. Stella and I had just been married and we used to hang with the Corwins now and then. I remember the four of us sat in Bob's apartment and watched the election returns the night JFK beat Nixon to the White House. Corwin was a song maven and a marvelous piano player. He was caught up in writing melodies, and his idols at the time included Richard Rodgers, Meredith Willson, and Henry Mancini. The two of us spent time analyzing these songs and discussing compositional tricks and tactics.

I took a shot at writing lyrics to a couple of Bob's melodies. I showed the lyrics to my new friend Alfred Uhry, who was at that time a full-time lyric writer. Alfred's advice was, "Don't write as if you're trying to write a song lyric." Wow, that turned me around. Bob Corwin and Mandy moved to L.A. around that time, and I didn't see them for about a year.

In the meantime, I had acquired a TV set for the first time in my life, and I got hung up on watching the bullfights from Mexico, narrated and explained in English by Carlos Montalbán. I read a dozen books about bullfighting, and learned about the history and customs, knew the names of all the passes and maneuvers. I considered myself an aficionado. I was eager to witness a real corrida, so when Stella and I visited L.A. to see family members, we called Bob and Mandy, and we drove down to Tijuana to see Jaime Bravo and a couple other matadors kill some bulls. I saw two bulls killed, and I nearly fainted. I had only seen black-and-white movies of the corrida, always with Montalbán's thoughtful and critical commentary. I was not prepared for the blood and violence. The second bull was slaughtered in a shameful manner, and the crowd was booing and screaming epithets at the toreros. "Let's go, quickly!" I said, and we four pale gringos hotfooted it back to the car and roared back to California. I never mentioned bullfighting after that. I was totally horrified.

Corwin called me the next day and we drove to Johnny Mercer's home in Brentwood. Bob had agreed to feed the dogs and water the plants while the Mercers were out of town. I saw the original work sheets for classic songs like "Come Rain or Come Shine" and "Out of This World," and I was fascinated to see what Harold Arlen had scratched out, and the different lyric ideas that Mercer had considered. As I remember, there was a wall with framed examples of these work sheets.

Blossom Dearie was the one who subsequently introduced me to Johnny Mercer in New York, and he was very complimentary about certain of my songs and once sent me a postcard saying, "You are my favorite lyric writer at the moment, but, BOY, are you uncommercial!!!" Once he came into Eddie Condon's in the Hotel Sutton where I was just getting off work, and suggested we go hear some good singer. I took him in a cab to the Apartment to hear Charles DeForest. Mercer was pretty well potted by this time. We sat down near the piano bar and ordered drinks, and Mercer noticed the woman singing at the keyboard. He was not impressed, and he said very loudly, "So? Is this what you wanted me to hear?" I conferred with DeForest, who quickly took over at the piano, and acknowledged Mercer's presence. DeForest announced that he would sing one of Mercer's lesser-known songs, and dived into it. Mercer stood up, put on his coat, and barked, "That's Leo Robin's lyric, for Christ's sake," and walked out into the night, leaving me with the drinks and the tab. Mercer came into Condon's again later that week, and had only a dim recollection of the DeForest episode.

I sat with him and Blossom at the Village Gate one night; Blossom was appearing there, and the other act was sitars and tablas just wailing away at high volume, and Mercer had to talk loudly to make conversation at our table. Finally he shouted at these Indian players, "Didn't you guys ever hear of swing? One-two-three-four?" I had to laugh—it was a Thurber cartoon.

I ran into Mercer years later when I was playing for Irene Kral at Diamante's in Hollywood and Mercer came in to hear her. My parents were visiting L.A. at the time, and Joyce Collins and I were sitting with them in the nightclub. Mercer came over to our table and was very gracious in his greeting to me, and of course I was proud to introduce him to Joyce and my mother and dad. Later, when we left the club, I asked my dad if he had enjoyed the music. His reply was typical,

"It's not my cup of tea." Then he added, "Your friend Mercer. You can't argue with that kind of success."

A Party for Red

One of the incidental gigs I did with Ben Webster was a private party at the Hotel Theresa in Harlem that began at 1 a.m. It was a welcome home party for Red Dillon, a notorious underworld guy who apparently was a respected figure in Harlem. Ben explained to me that, months before, Red had been kidnapped by rival gangsters, beaten savagely, and left for dead on a country road. Ben told me, "Everyone thought he had died, but he survived, and he's making his first appearance here tonight, and all these people are here to cheer and wish him well. Roll your coat up and stuff it in the bass drum case. If you have to go to the men's room, tell me and I'll go with you. Red's got a lot of friends, and he's also got a lot of enemies. They tried to kill this man, and they may try to kill him again. Ready? 'Blues in G.'"

Red walked in about 2 a.m., surrounded by several guys in coats and hats. He was a wiry little man, reminded me of Sammy Davis a little. It was apparent that he had been through a hell of an ordeal. As I remember, he was walking with a cane. The guests at the party were well-dressed black men, accompanied by spectacular ladies, most of them Caucasian. The party was over in a couple of hours, and that was the end of the Red Dillon episode. Or so I thought.

About ten years later, I was living in Los Angeles and playing frequently at Donte's in North Hollywood. One night I was hanging out in the backyard at Donte's, swapping Ben Webster stories with a few of the regulars, and I mentioned the party for Red Dillon, and a guy named Smitty piped up, "You were there? I was there! And you won't believe this, but Red is in town right now, and I'm going to tell him about this. He'll love it!"

The next night Smitty walked in with Red Dillon, who looked to be in great shape. We shook hands. Red didn't remember me specifically, but he said the party at the Hotel Theresa was a big moment in his life. He said, "Lemme buy you a taste." We toasted Ben Webster, and Red said, "I want to thank you for playing at my party." I told him I had a wonderful time.

About a week later, Smitty came into Donte's, took me aside and told me, "They whacked Red. They did him in yesterday afternoon." All I could do was gulp. I pulled a long face and said solemnly, "Wow, that's a drag." "It certainly is," Smitty said. "He owed me quite a bit of money." I told Smitty I thought Red seemed like a very nice guy. Smitty nodded and said, "He had his moments."

Studs Terkel

I met Studs once. I was playing at Rick's Cafe Americain in Chicago, and somebody set up a live radio interview for me with Studs. It was in the morning in the studios of Chicago's NPR station. I showed up on time, stepped out of the elevator, and there was Studs Terkel, saying "Are you Mr. Frishberg? Follow me, and I hope to God somebody remembered to leave the studio open, because I haven't got my keys with me. These people don't know who I am, and they don't pay attention to me. Studio A. Locked tight. You and I are in trouble, Mr. Frishberg. Let's try these other doors, but that's not gonna work, I guarantee we're locked out. Typical. Typical. Fifty years in this business, and this is the situation they put me into—locked out of the damn studio. Glad YOU got here on time, 'cause nobody else showed up! ANYBODY HOME HERE?"

At that point a guy walked up with a coffeepot and a bag of donuts and said, "Morning Studs, we're ready to go." Studs said, "Here's my engineer. Hi, Donald. It's just me and Mr. Frishberg today." And we

Before a gig at Nick's Tavern in the Village on the corner of Tenth Street and Seventh Avenue, New York City, located around the corner from my apartment. (Left to right) Buzzy Drootin, Jack Six, me, Cutty Cutshall, and Kenny Davern. (Personal collection)

With Monty Budwig (left) and Nick Ceroli (center). (Personal collection)

Before my performance at the Blue Wisp in Cincinnati. (Dan Carraco)

With the Bob Crosby Orchestra, Freedomland, CA. (Personal collection)

Dave:

Thanks. How did I ever get on your mailing list? You are my favorite lyric writer at the moment, but, BOY, are you uncommercial!!! However, I suppose you know that. Congratulation and my gratitude. Okla. Toad and W. & D. are marvellous.

Johnny Mercer

Letter from Johnny Mercer. (Personal collection)

Favorite photos taken by my good friend Bob Daugherty. (Bob Daugherty)

With lyricists and singers Bob Dorough and Jon Hendricks in New York City. (Personal collection)

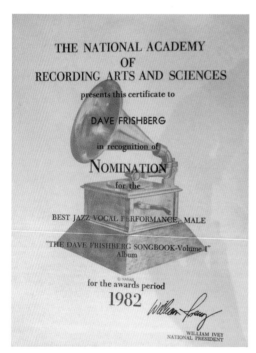

Grammy nomination for Best Jazz Vocal Performance—Male, 1982. (Personal collection)

Recognized by the Jazz Society of Oregon with the Golden Note Award in 2000. (Personal collection)

The American Society of Composers, Authors and Publishers
proudly inscribes into the Jazz Wall of Fame the name of

DAVE FRISHBERG

Marilyn Bergman
President & Chairman, ASCAP

June 1, 2007   New York City

My name inscribed in the ASCAP Jazz Wall of Fame. (Personal collection)

Finally made it in my adopted hometown, Portland, OR. Inducted into the Oregon Music Hall of Fame in 2008. (Personal collection)

OREGON MUSIC HALL OF FAME

DAVID FRISHBERG

2nd ANNUAL INDUCTION CEREMONY

2008

The love of my life, my wife, April Magnusson. I owe it all to her!
(Personal collection)

With April in Monterey, CA, circa 1992.
(Personal collection)

Hanging out with David Rosner, my good friend
and music publisher. (Personal collection)

walked right into the studio. The door wasn't locked at all. We sat down at our mics, and the interview began. We were live on the radio. I had the feeling that he had no idea who I was or what I did, and I was a little uneasy, because we hadn't had any conversation yet, just Studs muttering and complaining and acting panicky.

"My guest is jazz pianist Dave Frishberg. So. You're appearing for two weeks at Rick's Cafe Americain. Last time you were here was at the Gate of Horn with Odetta. Isn't that right? Tell me, what do think of Jess Stacy?" And that's how the interview began.

I got a tape of the interview. I remember that Studs did most of the talking, and we drifted off into topics that I never dreamed we would be discussing. He was very well informed and knowledge-able about swing music and classic jazz, although I didn't agree with some of his musical judgments. He was ready to argue, too. What a character.

Several years later I read a piece in the *New Yorker* about Studs Terkel's radio show. It told how Studs liked to put the guest a little on edge before he went on the air. His favorite tactic was to act confused and thwarted, as if he were unsure of what he was doing. Apparently Studs felt that the interview often went better if the guest were caught unawares and taken by surprise.

Six

Dear Bix (notes)

Dear Bix

Bix, old friend,
Are you ever going to comprehend
You're no ordinary standard B-flat run-of-the-mill-type guy?
Oh my, no

And Bix, old elf,
Will you ever learn to look at yourself
Like the others around you who love you and never ask why?

And seriously, Bix, old bear,
Don't you dig that big blue sky up there? Admit it,
Wouldn't it be nice to cut yourself a slice of that pie up there?

I wonder, Bix, old chum,
When you reminisce in years to come
Will you ever hum that someday song
You've been looking so long to find?

So do what you got to do
And may the years be good to you
'Cause you're one of the favored few, dear Bix,

You're one of a kind.

One morning I was driving alone up the coast highway to Santa Barbara, and I stopped in Malibu to visit Johnny Mandel. We had discussed writing a song together, and I had told him I would write a lyric and submit it to him, but weeks later I still didn't have the slightest idea what to write about. I promised him that morning I'd get to work on it.

When I resumed driving, I listened to a cassette of 1920s recordings by Paul Whiteman's orchestra featuring Bix Beiderbecke on cornet and Hoagy Carmichael on both piano and vocals. I had recently enjoyed rereading Hoagy's book *The Stardust Road*, all about his escapades at Indiana University, how he met and befriended Beiderbecke, and how he discovered that jazz music was indeed shaping his own life. I had first read the book when I was fifteen years old. I thought it was beautifully written, and it made a big impression on me.

As I listened in the car, I remembered a scene in the book where Hoagy and Bix, high as kites, are listening to Stravinsky's *Firebird* on the phonograph and talking seriously about their musical dreams. An idea for a lyric hit me: Hoagy would say, "Wouldn't it be nice to cut yourself a slice of that pie?" And the lyric took off from there. By the time I reached Santa Barbara, I had practically the whole lyric planned, or at least the first draft of it.

Driving back the next day, I stopped in Malibu and dropped the lyric, titled "Dear Bix," on Mandel's desk. A few days later, Mandel had a lead sheet ready to show me. I loved the piano intro he made— quoting from Bix's composition "In a Mist." But I wasn't drawn to the melody he had devised for the "Hoagy" character to sing.

In retrospect, I'm shocked by my chutzpah. I called Johnny Mandel and told him that I had a different feeling in mind, and that I had decided to write the melody myself. "Can I use your intro?" I asked him. "Of course," Mandel said. "It's not mine anyhow—it's Beiderbecke's passage." A week later, when I played the song for him, Mandel was gracious; he said, "That's good, but I still like mine better."

Thirty-five years later, Mandel and I chatted in the lobby of the Algonquin, where I had just sung "Dear Bix" in the Oak Room. Mandel said, "You were right about the Bix song. Mine didn't have that 'period' feel to it." I told him I still felt awkward about evaluating his composition. He replied, "Awkward is okay."

~

In 1980 I was in the cast of a Hoagy Carmichael musical at the Mark Taper Forum in Los Angeles. The show, written by Adrian Mitchell, a prominent English poet and playwright, was based on *The Stardust Road* and included elaborate stagings of about twenty classic Carmichael songs. Bix Beiderbecke was one of the two main characters. Dick Sudhalter played the Bix cornet solos and was the musical director. I was naturally struck by the fact that my song "Dear Bix" seemed to have been written expressly for this very same story, this very same script, but something told me to keep my mouth shut.

During one early rehearsal Hoagy Carmichael, now a crusty guy in his mid-eighties, showed up, and I saw a chance to play my Hoagy song for the man himself. Surely he would understand; after all, it's about him and Bix and college days in Bloomington, for Chrissake. I took him into a small rehearsal room with a spinet, and without a word of explanation I played and sang "Dear Bix." When I finished, Hoagy said, "Nice. Excuse me, I better get going," and he was out the door.

As for me, I was relieved that I hadn't tried to install one of my songs into Hoagy's show. You know what I mean?

After the opening night, I attended the party for the cast, crew, and band. Hoagy was there, drink in hand, convivial and complimentary to all the actors and musicians. "You haven't got a lot of vocal power," he told me, "but I could understand every word, and that's what counts."

Adrian Mitchell arrived, and Hoagy announced, "Here's the author!" Then he stood face-to-face with Mitchell, waving a finger at Adrian's nose, and he said, "You just didn't get it, did ya! I'm talking about my book! You didn't even come close, did ya!" The director steered Hoagy off to meet someone else, and Adrian stood there in shock. That episode pretty well stopped the celebration. Sudhalter and I walked to the parking lot, and there stood Adrian in tears. "I'm going back to London as soon as I can get a flight out," he told us.

The show didn't get good reviews, and it ran for the scheduled month. The band (onstage) was excellent, the cast was excellent, and everybody got along. I had the time of my life, had a few lines, sang four Hoagy songs from the piano, and did a choreographed routine with Amanda McBroom while clutching a French horn. Don't ask.

Years later, when Sudhalter was writing his biography of Carmichael, we talked about *The Stardust Road*, and how memorable and influential that book had been for both of us. "Remember the cast party?" he asked me. "Hoagy was right, don't you agree?" I knew precisely what he was talking about. "I'm afraid so," I said.

Seven

Schoolhouse Rock

I'm Just a Bill

Narrator:
Whew! You sure gotta climb a lot of steps to get to the Capitol
Building here in Washington. Hey, I wonder who that sad little scrap of
paper is . . .

BILL [sings]:
I'm just a bill, yes I'm only a bill
And I'm sittin' here on Capitol Hill.
Well it's a long long journey to the capital city,
It's a long long wait while I'm sittin' in committee,
But I know I'll be a law some day.
'Least I hope and pray that I will,
But today I am still just a bill.

Narrator:
Gee, Bill, you certainly have a lot patience and courage.

BILL [speaks]:
Well, I got this far. When I started, I wasn't even a bill—I was just an idea.

Some folks back home decided they wanted a law passed, so they called
their local congressman, and he said, "You're right, there ought to be a
law!" Then he sat down and wrote me out and introduced me to Congress,

153

and I became a bill. And I'll remain just a bill until they decide to make me a law.

BILL [*sings*]:
I'm just a bill, yes I'm only a bill
And I got as far as Capitol Hill.
Now I'm in committee, and I'll sit here and wait
while a few key congressmen discuss and debate
Whether they should let me be a law.
How I hope and pray that they will
But today I am still just a bill.

[Sound of jabbering voices under]

Narrator:
Listen to those congressmen arguing! Is all that discussion and debate about you?

BILL [*speaks*]:
Yeah, I'm one of the lucky ones. Most bills never even get this far. I hope they decide to report on me favorably. Otherwise I may die.

Narrator:
Die!

BILL [*speaks*]:
Yeah, die in committee. [Voices rise to a cheer] But it looks like I'm gonna live. Now I go to the House of Representatives and they vote on me.

Narrator:
If they vote yes, what happens?

Bill [speaks]:
Then I go to the Senate and the whole thing starts all over again.

Narrator:
Oh no!

BILL [speaks]:
Oh yes!

BILL [sings]:
I'm just a bill, yes I'm only a bill
And if they vote for me on Capitol Hill
Well then I'm off to the White House
Where I wait in a line
With a lot of other bills
For the president to sign,
And if he signs me, then I'll be a law.
How I hope and pray that he will,
But today I am still just a bill.

Narrator:
You mean even if the whole Congress says you should be a law—the president can still say no?

BILL [speaks]:
Yes, that's called a veto. If the president vetoes me, I have to go back to the Congress and they vote on me again. But by that time . . .

Narrator:
By that time it's very unlikely that you'll become a law. It's not easy to become a law, is it?

BILL [speaks]:
No.

BILL [*sings*]:
But how I hope and pray that I will.
But today I am still
Just a bill.

Narrator:
Good luck, Bill.

BILL [*speaks*]:
Thanks. I'm gonna need it.

Words and music by Dave Frishberg for the ABC series *Schoolhouse Rocks*
© 1973 American Broadcasting Music, Inc.

I'm Just a Bill

"I'm Just a Bill," written for the *Schoolhouse Rock* series on ABC, turns out to be my most well-known song. Bob Dorough was the musical director of the series, wrote nearly all of the songs, arranged and produced all the musical tracks, and sang on most of them.

There's nothing musical that Bob Dorough can't accomplish, and a Bob Dorough accomplishment is always sound musically, always original and fresh, and no matter what the category may be—jazz, symphonic, baroque, choral, country, medieval, or songs for kids—it is all conceived with utmost ingenuity and unrivaled craftsmanship, and with a passion that gleams from everything he puts his mind and heart to. He is primarily a pianist, but he can play just about any instrument he picks up. He's a skillful singer as a soloist, or with vocal groups, choirs, and glee clubs. He is a magnetic performer onstage and on recordings. He's also an inspired lyric writer, one of the best of his generation. In short, he's the most remarkably talented musician I've ever known, and certainly the most prolific artist.

"What are you working on now?" can be a perplexing query when posed to a creative artist. A common reply is, "I'm about to begin such and such," or, "I'm planning to do this or that." Dorough tells you what he's just finished. He's churning something out every week, every day; there's no stopping him.

When *Schoolhouse Rock* took off in the early 1970s, and needed new material quickly, Bob began to farm out some of the assignments to other writers, including me, who by then had moved to Los Angeles. "I'm Just a Bill" was the first song I wrote for the series.

Dorough came out to Los Angeles to record two *Schoolhouse Rock* songs: "Conjunction Junction" and "I'm Just a Bill." I was working regularly then with Jack Sheldon, and I wrote the role of the scrap of paper with Jack's voice in mind. The narrator's part was played by Jack's eleven-year-old son, John Jr.

The band was composed of jazz players including Sheldon on trumpet, Teddy Edwards on saxophone, me and Dorough on keyboards, Leroy Vinnegar on bass, Bill Goodwin on drums, and Stuart Scharf on guitar. The two songs we recorded that afternoon would become the flagship songs of *Schoolhouse Rock*.

I wouldn't be surprised if many people were to regard "I'm Just a Bill" as my most important piece of work. Monetarily speaking, they're probably correct.

George Newall, along with Radford Stone, was the producer of *SR*, and he was a fan of my songs, and a smart editor of my work. Tom Yohe was the artistic designer for the series. Tom was a brilliant cartoonist and animator, and his characters and images caught the essence and spirit of each idea that each songwriter proposed.

Of course Newall had to run the writers' ideas past the ABC executives, and the network folks were primarily concerned with the "tutorial" element of each topic, and they wanted to make sure the educational content of the *SR* productions measured up to their standards. When I submitted "Walkin' on Wall Street," a song about investing in the stock market, Newall showed my scenario to the ABC, folks who replied with the most peculiar criticism I have ever been faced with. "Tell Mr. Frishberg," they said, "that he has neglected to mention dollar cost averaging."

I told George to tell ABC that references to dollar cost averaging are conspicuously absent in all the songs I write. That's my gimmick. But I was happy to comply, and Dorough shined a light on the event with his orchestration. It turned out that "Walkin' on Wall Street," my tribute to capitalism, is my favorite *Schoolhouse Rock* concoction. I played Lester the Investor, and drummer Grady Tate took the part of Leroy the Adviser.

Walkin' on Wall Street

NEWSBOY *[speaks]:*
Get your paper here! Latest Wall Street prices and stock market reports!

LESTER *[speaks]:*
Hey, I'll take one of those! Here's a quarter, keep the change.

LESTER *[sings]:*
You got to be cool
When you're walkin' on Wall Street
Like goin' to school
You learn a lot every day
And this is the rule
When you're walkin' on Wall Street
Buy low sell high take a piece of the pie
That's the Wall Street way.

NARRATOR [speaks]:

When you use your money to make more money, that's called an investment.
When you invest in a corporation, that means you own a part of it.

LESTER [sings]

The companies that manufacture things we use
Like telescopes and videos and high-top shoes
Are looking for investors such as me and you
So we can own shares in the company too.

NARRATOR [speaks]:

That's called stock. Smart investors look to buy stock in a company that's going
up in value.

LESTER [sings]

Here's a stock that's looking mighty good I think
Whiz Bang Kola (that's my favorite drink)
Looks as if their sales are going up sky-high
Better call my broker
And instruct him to buy

LESTER [speaks]:

Hello, Leroy? This is Lester the Investor. Whiz Bang Kola's going up. Buy some
stock for me.

LEROY [on phone]:

Okay, Lester, confirming your order. Buy Whiz Bang Kola at eight and a
quarter.

LESTER [sings]:

You gotta be smart
When you're walkin' on Wall Street
So just for a start
I check the paper each day.

First I read the comics, then I check the sports,
And then I take a look at the market reports
To see if my stock is ridin' low or high
So I know when to sell and I know when to buy.

[Lester notices Whiz Bang stock is down.]

LESTER *[speaks]:*
[to Newsboy] Here's a dime, keep the change.

LESTER *[speaks]:*
Stock prices go up and down, so smart investors like me buy a little at a
time every month. That way the ups and downs average out in the long run.
Leroy calls that "dollar cost averaging."

LESTER *[sings]:*
I don't wanna get hurt
When I'm walkin' on Wall Street.
I could lose my shirt,
Not to mention my case,
So I stay alert
When I'm walkin' on Wall Street.
Buy low, sell high, take a piece of the pie . . .

NEWSBOY *[speaks]:*
Read all about it! Latest Wall Street flash!
Whiz Bang Kola is on the rise!

LESTER [sings]:
Well I came out ahead
And I'm swingin' on Wall Street
And just like I said
I'm learning more every day
So I remember the rule
When you're walkin' on Wall Street.
Buy low, sell high, take your piece of the pie
That's the Wall Street Way

[to NEWSBOY] Here's a dollar, keep the change
Now you're walkin' on Wall Street!

Words and music by Dave Frishberg for the ABC series *Schoolhouse Rock*
© 1997 American Broadcasting Music, Inc.

Eight

The Hopi Way

The Hopi Way

I'm from the old school
The proper and the prude school
Where it's stiff upper lip, stay quietly hip
And never reveal what you feel

Behold now the new school
The recently tattooed school
Where it's "in your face," and crank up the bass
And climb to the top of the pile
I prefer a much lower profile
For my style

I could bring a big sound blaster
Sing louder, play faster
That's a recipe for sure disaster
A catastrophe
'Cause it wouldn't be the Hopi way

I could wear a small gold earring
Make phone calls while steering
I could boogie till I lose my hearing
Not my cuppa tea
'Cause it wouldn't be the Hopi way

Wouldn't be the Hopi way
To be loud, to be crude
To be raw, to be rude for the sake of just saying my say
But hey!

If that's the way they want to play it
My scruples outweigh it
And that is why I must nay-nay it
Though it may be the game of the day
I don't want to play
'Cause it wouldn't be the Hopi way . . .

II

I'm from the old school
And that's my alma mater
Where you button your coat, you don't rock the boat,
And "don't blow your cool" is the rule.
(more)

As opposed to the new school
Where temperaments run hotter.
Where they taunt and gloat and go for the throat
And put their opponents to shame
But you know that was never the name
Of my game.

I cannot deny I'd love it
To tell them to shove it
But still I must remain above it
That's barbarity
And it wouldn't be the Hopi way

I could so succinctly say it
Two short words convey it
But clearly I could not okay it
That's vulgarity
And it wouldn't be the Hopi way

Wouldn't be the Hopi way
To be cold, to be cruel
And use that as a tool for the sake of just making my day
No way . . .

So I've decided I won't sweat it
The new school? Forget it
But don't forget to give me credit
Even though I'm no Hopi per se
That's the part I play
'Cause that would be the Hopi way.

That would be the Hopi way [chant fades out]

Words and music by Dave Frishberg
© 2002 Swiftwater Music ASCAP

The Old School

This started out as an idea for a song to be called "The Old School," and the first thing I wrote down was "I'm from the old school and that's my alma mater." I guess I was thinking of it as a song I could fit into my concert program as a kind of survey of my offerings.

For years I've been using the expression "not Hopi way" (emphasis on *way*) when answering common questions like, "Are you wearing a tie tonight?" or, "More potatoes?"

I may have heard this expression in a movie. A noble chief, who refuses to act in a dishonorable way, says solemnly, "Not Hopi way." Or maybe John Wayne said it. But I may have made it up.

The Hopi way is essentially outmoded. It's stubborn adherence to forgotten and obsolete values. To say one will follow the Hopi way is to say, "I'm going to live on the fringes of society." (Dancing to a different tom-tom).

I tried out the song for the first time during an engagement at the Algonquin in 2002 and was greeted with puzzled applause. I did a major rewrite since then. Originally the song lacked focus and ended in a puzzling way. Now I know what tone to take and what the song is about. It's about me, personally, mocking myself (but not unkindly) about being stubborn and close-minded. I try not to write lyrics about myself, especially in my own voice, but this one feels useful as an opener because it characterizes my program and my attitude and helps to frame the songs. If it doesn't get laughs, though, I know I'm in for a rough night.

Music and the Bing Hu Generation

When I was young I was proud to call myself a musician. Today, admitting you're a musician leaves you vulnerable to being classified as "talented." Once the faintest of compliments, the word *talented* has sunk even lower, and now it is routinely used to describe an aptitude similar to one's own.

Am I a musician? Not necessarily. I am offended by the cheapening of the word *musician* as applied to practitioners of pop music. Michael Jackson may be a genius dancer and a charismatic entertainer, but when I hear him referred to as a "musician" I slump in disappointment. If Michael Jackson is a musician, then what's the word for André Previn or Yo-Yo Ma or Itzhak Perlman or Duke Ellington or Stan Getz? Don't answer; I don't want to know.

Music has lost its essence as an artistic form, and is becoming more and more an expression of one's identity, one's image and attitude, and even one's relevance to society. A person now may decide to become a "musician" not because he's responding to some persistent musical imperative, but because music is easy. I think people today see music as a path to notoriety and respect, an ideal showcase to display one's qualifications for celebrity, now that celebrity has become the goal of practically all popular artistic endeavor.

Music becomes the way you exercise power. Power and authority through music may be expressed by high decibels (music as bludgeon); by racking up megamillions in profits (music as cash cow); or by creating an environment that's dominated by music playing everywhere all the time (music as pollutant).

Practically everyone is talented in some way—intellectually, mechanically, athletically, mathematically, and certainly musically. There are millions of us who know how to strum and pick guitars, toot horns, bang drums, manipulate keyboards, and sing with passionate abandon. I was about to say that music has replaced baseball as our National Pastime, but I think it's more accurate to say that "talent" has become our National Obsession.

Nine

Van Lingle Mungo

Van Lingle Mungo

Heeney Majeski, Johnny Gee
Eddie Joost, Johnny Pesky, Thornton Lee
Danny Gardella
Van Lingle Mungo

Whitey Kurowski, Max Lanier
Eddie Waitkus and Johnny Vander Meer
Bob Estalella
Van Lingle Mungo

Augie Bergamo, Sigmund Jakucki
Big Johnny Mize and Barney McCosky
Hal Trosky

Augie Galan and Pinky May
Stan Hack and Frenchy Bordagaray
Phil Cavarretta, George McQuinn
Howie Pollett and Early Wynn
Art Passarella
Van Lingle Mungo

John Antonelli, Ferris Fain
Frankie Crosetti, Johnny Sain
Harry Brecheen and Lou Boudreau
Frankie Gustine and Claude Passeau
Eddie Basinski
Ernie Lombardi
Hughie Mulcahy
Van Lingle . . . Van Lingle Mungo

Words and music by Dave Frishberg

The National Pastime

E-mails to and from Jim Charlton, August 2006

Dave—

Have you ever updated "Van Lingle Mungo," maybe not for recording but just playing around? I ask because I was thinking that if you had it would make a very nice one-page article in the *National Pastime*. I was delighted to hear you in NYC a few years ago when you were at the Century Club.

Jim Charlton

Publications Director

Society for American Baseball Research

Jim—

Thanks for your note. Re "VLM," I've never considered updating the song, because I think of it as a string of names intended to generate a feeling of nostalgia, whether or not the listener recognizes the baseball connection. "Updating" the song might tend to wipe out its essential character.

For instance—after a concert about twenty-five years ago in Seattle, a guy said to me, "I love the song you sang with all the names of your childhood friends." "Wow!" I thought, "that's it! My childhood friends—that's the mood I'm after, all right." And I was about to congratulate the guy on being such a keen listener, but he continued: "You know, one of those guys was a baseball player."

And that stopped me in my tracks, because it proved—to me, anyway—that the song was not about baseball per se, but more about childhood memories, mundane and trivial maybe, but powerful in a curious way.

Here's a piece about "Van Lingle Mungo" for *The National Pastime*:

In 1969, I was working as a pianist in New York City and beginning to write songs. I composed a rather brooding piece in what I considered a "bossa nova" style—a wide-ranging melodic line and a wandering tonal center. I had equipped the melody with two different lyrics. One was an angry satirical verse titled "Dear Mister Nixon"; the other was called "Don't Look Behind You" and soberly implored the listener to face the future. Neither lyric seemed to match the ambitious melody line.

One night I was paging through the newly published MacMillan *Baseball Encyclopedia* and my eyes fell on the name Van Lingle Mungo. "VAN LINGLE MUNGO"—the name scanned perfectly with a recurring melodic figure in my song, and I instantly sang it out loud. I knew then that the lyric would be only names—not names of famous stars, but names that evoked my childhood memories, and, incidentally, illuminated some fragments of forgotten baseball history. I dived into the book, assembling names that scanned, rhymed, and related loosely to those years, the years of my childhood passion for the game. Within an hour or so I had a complete lyric.

About a month later I recorded an album of my songs, including "Mungo," and that turned out to be the only track that got any airplay. I was surprised. But I always felt the lyric wasn't finished, it wasn't doing the job, and I kept tinkering with it. In my opinion, I improved the song. I took out certain names from the original lyric and replaced them with names from an earlier (wartime) era so that the nostalgic focus might be sharper. Johnny Kucks and his rhyme mate Virgil Trucks had to go and were replaced by Lou Boudreau and Claude Passeau, whose names certainly sang better. The replacement of Roy Campanella's conveniently rhyming name was necessary because he was too recent.

So I changed it to Art Pasarella (an umpire), and that seemed to do the job: Gardella, Pasarella, and Estalella.

Then I learned that Bob Estalella's name didn't rhyme in the first place, because it was pronounced as in Spanish: Esta-leya. So the whole rhyme scheme should have been scrapped, starting with "Danny Gardella," and now I stand forever humiliated in Baseball Songland. What did I know? I grew up in a minor-league town and never heard Estalella's name uttered, only saw it in print. Same goes for Johnny Gee, whose name I mangled on the record with a soft *g*. There may be other names I'm mispronouncing, but at this stage further corrections would only confuse me.

In my search for relevant names that scanned, "John Antonelli" was an unfortunate choice, and it's annoying that he's in the song, because there turns out to be two John Antonellis whose major-league careers nearly overlapped. I was thinking of the third baseman who was up briefly with the Cardinals and Braves during the war; I had seen him play with Columbus. I wasn't even aware of the more famous Johnny Antonelli, the left hander for the Giants. By the time Antonelli No. 2 came along, I had already traded Duke Snider for Duke Ellington.

If you are keeping track, there are currently four surviving players from the Mungo song. I confirmed the dates of demise on a website called The Baseball Almanac, wherein biographical and statistical data claimed to be updated as of March 1, 2005. Of the original thirty-eight names, the surviving Mungolians are Joost, Sain, Pesky, and Basinski.

(*Author's note:* As of October 2016, Basinski was the sole survivor.)

I'm positive Eddie Basinski is still alive and well, because he lives here in Portland, Oregon, and enjoys considerable celebrity and adulation as a Portland Beaver immortal. I had occasion to meet him once, and I excitedly told him how I used to watch him with the St. Paul Saints in 1946. "You and Gene Mauch were a great double-play combination," I blurted. Basinski frowned and said, "Mauch wasn't much help."

Then I told him, "You're in my song, you know."

"Your song?"

"Yes, have you ever heard my song 'Van Lingle Mungo'?"

Basinski stepped back, stared at me as if I were from Mars, excused himself, and walked off to chat with someone else.

The only other guy from the song I ever met was Mungo himself, who arrived from Pageland, South Carolina, to be on *The Dick Cavett Show* and listen to me sing the song. This was 1969, when Cavett had a nightly show in New York. Backstage, Mungo asked me, "When do I get the first check?" When he heard my explanation about how there was unlikely to be any remuneration for anyone connected with the song, least of all him, he was genuinely downcast.

"But it's my name," he said.

I told him, "The only way you can get even is to go home and write a song called Dave Frishberg."

He laughed, and when we said goodbye he said, "I'm gonna do it! I'm gonna do it!"

If he did it, the *Baseball Almanac* doesn't mention it.

Dave,

This is a nice piece. We have an issue in the spring devoted entirely to "individuals in the game" and this would fit perfectly. The only thing I think missing is the lyrics. Would it be okay to run those as well?

Hello Jim,

Attached herewith is a PDF (Acrobat) file of "Van Lingle Mungo," formatted exactly as I would like it. I spoke to the publisher about permission, and he asked that you use the copyright attribution as indicated. Before publication, I would ask you to send me a proof of the lyrics as they will appear.

By the way, I have found Art Passarella's name occasionally spelled with one *s*, and I'm not sure which is correct—one or two *s*'s. I have decided not to lose any sleep over it.

Thanks,

DF

Dave,

Just a quick glance but I know that Cavarretta is misspelled and Vander Meer has a break in his name. I assume it is okay to change those when we get to that point.

Jim

Jim—

Thanks for spotting these errors. After all these years, despite my self-righteous campaign of revisions and corrections, to discover that the song is still riddled with flaws—this is a cruel blow indeed. Will these revelations never cease? You're right, *Cavarretta* and *Vander Meer* must be corrected. Please make the changes as needed.

This, then, is Mungo's Revenge. That night at the Cavett show I should have slipped Mungo a taste when he asked me about money.

Dave Frishberg

Alternate scenario

Dave—

Have you ever updated "Van Lingle Mungo"?

Jim—

Certainly not. I never dated him in the first place.

Ten

Matty

Matty

HEYWOOD BROUN [sings]:
When baseball was my beat, I was privileged to meet Christy
Mathewson. He was my friend, right-hander for the Giants when the
Game was still a science. Well, he's passed away, and it's safe to say
We'll never see the likes of him again

Now the truth is mighty and shall prevail.
And the inside game's passé.
So need I ask?
Brother, pass that flask
And we'll drink to Christy Mathewson today. . . .

(chorus)
You were great, Matty; there's not a soul who would deny that you were great.
When our luck was running sour, when our backs were to the wall,
You could fire up the will to win and galvanize us all.
Bring on Baker, bring on Wagner, bring on Collins, bring 'em all!
Just give Mathewson the ball, and he'll come through.

And it was true, Matty,
When we were down to do or die, we'd look to you.
You would stand up tall and confident with calm and steady nerve;
You would summon up that extra you'd been keeping in reserve;
Then you'd fool 'em with the fade-away, and fan 'em with the curve.
You deserved the trust and faith we placed in you.

And your name
Will echo down the hallowed halls of fame.
And men will tell of how you played the game.
'Cause win or lose, Matty,
You stayed a champion just the same

And they'll recall
How Matty was the mightiest of them all.
As long as young men play with bat and ball,
They'll speak of you, Matty,
They'll remember you.

Yes, you were rare, Matty.
And when a miracle was needed you were there.
When Chicago filled the bases, and the crowd began to roar,
And the crucial game was on the line, and we couldn't let 'em score,

And when someone had to stand up straight
And get that ball across the plate,
I'd swear, Matty . . .
I'd swear that God himself had sent his right-hand man
To see us through
And it was you, Matty,
It was you.

Words and music by Dave Frishberg
© 1986, 2011 Swiftwater Music

Mathewson and Chase

In the winter of 2009 I was engaged by three Portland authors who had written a play about the Algonquin Hotel roundtable titled *Vitriol and Violets* (subsequently changed to *The New Yorkers*). They asked me to write songs to insert into the script. Among the characters was the journalist Heywood Broun, and the actor who played that role was the best singer in the cast. I was stumped trying to find something suitable for Heywood Broun to sing about. Researching Broun's life, I was stunned to find that he had once named the writer Damon Runyon and the baseball star Christy Mathewson as his favorite dinner and drinking companions. Christy Mathewson! This was an amazing discovery, because I had already written the very song that might express the specific sentiments of Heywood Broun.

Years earlier, for a theater project that never got off the ground, titled *The Catbird Seat*, I wrote a dramatic song, a tribute to Christy Mathewson. The song was called "Matty," and it was designed to be sung in 1919 by the desk clerk at the Sinton Hotel in Cincinnati, moments after Matty himself, the most beloved and celebrated sports hero of the day, had checked into the hotel. I really liked the song, and I was doubtful that there would ever be any use for it. Amazing! All I had to do was write an introduction to the song, so that it would fit smoothly into the Algonquin situation. I checked the *Baseball Encyclopedia* for the date of Mathewson's death. It was 1925, clearly the era of the Algonquin lunches. So I had Heywood Broun informing his friends at lunch that he was on his way to the funeral of his pal Matty, and glasses were raised around the table in a toast to the famous athlete. It worked beautifully, and the song turned out to be a highlight of the play, in no small measure due to the actor's marvelous delivery.

The Catbird Seat

CHASE [enters the lobby, sings]
Same old Cinci-Fuckin'-Nati!
Same loud yokels at the bar
Same siding salesman from Ashtabula
Shakin' dice at the counter
For a cheap cigar.

[Spoken]
Step aside my friend, let me shake 'em up!

[Shakes dice]

Listen to 'em rattle in the big leather cup.
Cigar's on me! Enjoy it, pal!

[Sung]
Same lounge lizards in the lobby.
Same rotarians on the make.
But tonight I see some plungers, I see some pikers,
I see some spenders, some spongers, some lucky strikers.
I got a hunch there's bound to be a bunch at stake.

Boys, tonight I got a feeling
I'm the guy who's gonna win.
So whoever's doing the dealing—
You can definitely deal me in.

Stand back, buddy, while I squeeze by.
Gonna grab my slab of that greenback pie.
I'm up to bat and the world is at my feet.
'Cause I'm in the catbird seat.

I'm in position to pick my spot.
Gonna make my strike while the iron's hot.
Ev'ry deuce and ace gonna fall in place so neat,
'Cause I'm in the catbird seat.

It's my time.
This is the moment I can't refuse.
And it's no crime.
It's simply heads I win, and tails you lose.

Lady Luck, you have met your match
I'm counting chickens before they hatch.
It'll be a breeze just to stroll down easy street,
'Cause I'm in the catbird seat
[Extended dance]

[Then turns to FRANKIE]

When opportunity comes and knocks,
We're all set in a front-row box.
It's guaranteed, and there ain't no need to cheat,
'Cause we're in the catbird seat.

Other suckers may lose their shirt,
But you and me, pal, we can't get hurt.
They're on the spot, and it's us they got to beat,
'Cause we're in the catbird seat.

It's our show,
And we're directing the whole routine.
And it's big dough
Places, please, for the jackpot scene.

And when it's time to divide the pot
They'll all wind up with doodly squat.
And we'll be there for the lion's share tout suite,
'Cause we're in the catbird seat.

We're in the catbird seat, pal.
We're in the catbird seat.

Words and music by Dave Frishberg
© 1986 Swiftwater Music

The Catbird Seat

I began writing the book *The Catbird Seat* in 1978–'79. What I had in mind was a musical comedy about Frankie and his girlfriend Eloise who travel back in time to unfix the 1919 World Series, and thereby become involved in the Mathewson/Chase relationship, the peculiar friendship between two famous ballplayers of the early 1900s: Christy Mathewson, the symbol of American sportsmanship, and Hal Chase, the crooked star who loses ball games for the benefit of gamblers. Apparently, the two superstars were cordial friends and mutual admirers, although Matty eventually pressed the charges that led to Chase's banishment from Organized Baseball. The crooked 1919 World Series, in my story, brings Mathewson and Chase together in a conflict of values. And wouldn't you know it—Eloise falls for Chase. Lots of songs, lots of fun, and a little anguish.

Chase sings and dances a couple of big numbers in *The Catbird Seat.* The title song is a dance production introducing Chase as he enters the hotel lobby.

Another scene I imagined takes place on the baseball field as the World Series is about to begin. Eddie Cicotte, the Chicago White Sox star pitcher, has agreed with gamblers to make sure his team loses this game. Now he is having a change of heart. He sings:

The Wife and the Kid

Cicotte:
I'm a fair guy, I'm a square guy,
A hundred and ten percenter all the way.
You know I bust my keester ev'ry day
For the wife and the kid.

I'm a game guy, I'm the same guy
The team can always count on in a clutch.
And now I have to bear down twice as much
For the wife and the kid.

I blush, I bleed,
See where gambling and greed have brought me.
The shock, the shame,
Dishonor to my name . . .
Life would never be the same
If they caught me.

But now there's no doubt I'll pitch my heart out.
'Cause I will not live my life out in disgrace.
And I can look my family in the face.
And I'll be proud that I did what I did
For the wife and the kid.

[HAL CHASE is lurking nearby and he sings to CICOTTE]

Now, Eddie.
You can stay strong for only so long.
Then the day will come to pack away your spikes.
You can't go on forever throwing strikes
For the wife and the kid.

Comes a time, pal, when it's no crime, pal,
To let a game or two go down the drain.
Knowing that you got a lot to gain
For the wife and the kid.

You blush, you bleed,
But, Eddie, you agreed you'd blow it.
You took ten grand,
I put it in your hand,
Now you gotta take a stand, and you know it. . . .

My friends are no fools.
They play by no rules.
So I strongly would suggest you acquiesce.
Call it accident insurance more or less.
'Cause accidents can happen, God forbid . . .

To the wife and the kid.

[Spoken]
Time to play ball, Eddie.

Words and music by Dave Frishberg
© 1986, 2011 Swiftwater Music

So I started to write the book, but I was very uncertain as to how the plot would proceed, and I decided I would write the songs and leave the playwriting to a professional playwright. L.A. was crawling with them. I met a young man who had written a couple of screenplays, and several episodes of a successful TV crime series. Like me, he was a fan of baseball history. Instead of showing him my unfinished script, I showed him about ten songs. He liked them, and he went straight to work on a new script. Unfortunately, the guy was thinking in a totally different mood. I had designed the songs for a comedy, and my collaborator's characters, aside from Hal Chase, didn't match the people in my songs at all. Instead, he came up with a dark David Mamet–like story, short on humor and not much fun. There was no point in continuing our partnership, and I pulled out. The playwright told me that if I ever again tried to mount a production of *The Catbird Seat* he would sue me to my grave (or however Mamet may have put it). I don't doubt that he would sue me. So that's why *The Catbird Seat* never happened.

My Baseball Collection

I have collected old sports books and periodicals for decades, and I own some rare items, including copies of *Baseball Magazine* from the early 1900s, and Reach *Baseball Guide*s from 1911 and 1932.

The most extraordinary item in my collection is a book by Christy Mathewson titled *Won in the Ninth*. It's juvenile fiction, certainly ghost-written, the first in a series known as The Matty Books. I came across it in 1978 in a tiny bookstore in Soquel, California, near Santa Cruz. I was astonished to see that it was signed by Mathewson himself. It's a presentation copy (numbered 24), so I assume it was signed around 1910, which is the date of publication. The guy in the bookstore didn't seem to know its value. He asked $20 for it. I took the book home and proudly shelved it. Now and then I would pull it out and admire the autograph. Then one day I sat down and began to read it.

The story is about collegiate baseball heroics. The names of the lads are altered in the crudest way so the youthful readers won't fail to get the point: Ty Cobb was "Ty Robb," John McGraw was "John McGrew," Hughie Jennings was "Hughie Jenkins," and so forth. The protagonist is a chap from California named Harold Case. Here's Christy Mathewson on "Harold (Hal) Case":

As a matter of fact, Harold, as they called him back home, was a really good fellow. He was very boyish looking for his eighteen years. He was a well built fellow, but modest and somewhat backward about pushing himself forward. His hair was brown and his features were good although no one would call him handsome. His eyes were light blue and clear, his mouth was firm . . . he was quick as a flash in any game he was familiar with, and he was graceful as a deer in motion. He could run almost as fast as a deer, too.

The story was not compelling, although I was struck by the irony of Christy Mathewson's admiration for Hal Chase in those days. He obviously thought enough of Chase to make him the hero of his first book. I turned to the inside front cover to admire the signature, and it was then, for the first time, that I noticed what was typed on the presentation sticker that Matty had signed:

PRESENTATION COPY No. 24.

Won in The Ninth
To Mr. Harold Case
with the Compliments of
Christy Mathewson

Further research showed that Chase had died in 1947 in a little town near Santa Cruz. So it turns out that I now own Hal Chase's personal copy of Matty's book. What a responsibility. The book will be included of course among my most prized possessions, and entombed with my body so that I can take it with me into the next world. It's just the Egyptian in my soul.

I sent the above article to several friends, including the novelist

Arthur Phillips, who replied with a question: "Does the whole book read so much like gay porn?" Well, Arthur—now that you mention it, yes. Hmmm.

But in the meantime, there's been some formal research. Could it be possible that the signature was not really Mathewson's signature? Another friend responded:

R. Plapinger Baseball Books
Ashland, OR

Hi Dave,

It was with great interest that I read your Hal Chase/Christy Mathewson story.

A couple of weeks ago, in a magazine called *Sports* [sic] *Collectors Digest*, someone named "Ron Keurajian" says, "Throughout the years, I have seen a few hundred Mathewson signatures for sale, of which maybe twenty-five were genuine." He goes on to discuss identifying characteristics, media that are more likely or unlikely to have legit Matty sigs, etc.

He also pays particular attention to books signed by Mathewson and even addresses the "presentation" plate—as yours has–and states his opinion that in spite of the presence of said plate, it's his feeling that most Mathewson signatures in *Won in the Ninth* were not hand-signed by Mathewson. He speculates that they were most likely "secretarial— done by an employee of either the publisher or Mathewson. Anyway—I sent him your scan, and here is his response: "Thanks for the scan, I do not believe that is a genuine Mathewson" . . .

For all I know, this guy is full of crap, and the only "real" Mathewson signatures are the ones in his collection. Then again . . . does he have anything to gain by saying a signature is not genuine when it actually is?

I don't really think this diminishes your story, either. In fact, it could enhance it (who was it that typed "Harold Case" on that presentation slip? Who, if not Matty, signed it?). And the book is a "find" regardless of whether the signature is actually Mathewson's. I guess I'm just sending this along as "food for thought," especially if/when the time comes when you or your heirs are inclined to try and sell the book. I should also say that "signed" presentation copies of *Won in the Ninth* (presented to others than "Chase," of course) have sold regularly in major sports auctions, and the legitimacy of the signatures has never been challenged.

Bobby Plapinger

~

To Bobby Plapinger—

I agree. The idea that the book came from Hal Chase's personal library—that's the part I like. I wonder if Chase considered the autograph might be "secretarial." Or maybe he tried to pass it off as genuine, but nobody was buying it . . .

Or here's a scene: Chase shows the book to Chick Gandil (another notorious crooked ballplayer of the time) "Look, Chick, I got Matty's autograph in this juvenile potboiler. What do you think it's worth?"

Gandil looks it over. "You mean you fell for this bullshit? That's not Mathewson's signature, any fool can see that. . . . You got outfoxed on this one, Chase. Besides, look at this—they couldn't even get your friggin' name right."

Eleven

You Are There

You Are There

In the evening
When the kettle's on for tea
An old familiar feeling settles over me
And it's your face I see,
And I believe that you are there

In a garden
When I stop to touch a rose
And feel the petals soft and sweet against my nose
I smile and I suppose
That somehow maybe you are there

When I'm dreaming
And I find myself awake without a warning
And I rub my eyes and fantasize, and all at once I realize
It's morning,
And my fantasy is fading like a distant star at dawn
My dearest dream is gone
I often think there's just one thing to do
Pretend the dream was true
And tell myself that you are there

You Are There

This was a tough one, and I'm glad I stuck with it, because it was like solving the Sunday *Times* puzzle. Mandel's melody is a nonstop cascade of eighth notes with no rests and only a couple of spots to take a breath. He played it for me on the piano, and my first thought was, "A jingle for a Chinese laundry?"

The first thing I did was try to find a title. The first title I launched was "Lady Lola," but that only led to a prankish point of view that didn't fit with the calm and thoughtful cadences Mandel had placed at the end of each stanza. Johnny had written a profound rhapsody, and it wouldn't make sense to equip it with flippant language. Forget Lola.

I then wrote a complete lyric called "Maybe Next Time," which contained these memorable lines: "We're not perfect, that's for sure, not squeaky clean and pure, like Mary Tyler Moore . . ." I played it for Mandel, and when I got to the Mary Tyler Moore line I stopped and said, "This isn't right—I can do better than this. Forget this." There was a long pause, and Johnny said, "Well? . . . I think you're right."

So I started over, this time with the "stakes raised," and I wrote down the opening words—*In the evening*. That set the stage for me: This is an older person—young people don't say "In the evening," and they don't refer to the teakettle. The teakettle suggests that this is an Englishwoman talking. In a calm, educated English way, she addresses an absent person who is, or was, dear to her. I left it at that, and I never explored the nature of her relationship to the absentee. Death wasn't foremost on my mind, although I considered it as a possibility. The lyric works for a male singer, of course, but it's practically all females who choose to perform it. Maybe there is some inherent feminine aspect to the words. Tea? Roses? It sure ain't Vince Lombardi talking. On the other hand, one never knows.

Mandel liked it; he called me the "problem solver," and he told me that several big-name lyricists had taken a crack at that melody and given up on it. In conversations with me, he sometimes refers to "You Are There" as the Mary Tyler Moore song.

The first recording of "You Are There" was by the actress Ruth Warrick, accompanied by pianist Mike Renzi, in a collection called *Phoebe Tyler Sings*, a reference to Warrick's role in *All My Children* on daytime TV. I couldn't have "cast" the song any better. She nailed that dreamy English lady just right. I was surprised when I learned she was from Missouri. Hey, that's called acting.

I've often seen and heard "You Are There" referred to as "a song about death," and I soon began to think of it that way myself. When I first began to sing it in public I was unable to finish the song without getting teary-eyed. But to me, the all-time best tearjerker has got be "Old Shep":

"And if there is a heaven where good doggies go, I know that Old Shep has a home."

You can't top that one, podner.

Twelve

Portland

Portland

In 1986 I was living in the San Fernando Valley in Los Angeles with my second wife and year-old son Harry. The jam-packed freeways drove me crazy and I knew it would soon be impossible for me to continue living in Los Angeles on my income as a jazz musician.

My manager booked some gigs for me in Portland, Oregon. I was instantly attracted to the beautiful city, with its affordable homes, the vibrant music scene, its laid-back lifestyle, and, best of all, less traffic. I decided to make the move to Portland and buy a house. My second son, Max, was born soon after the move.

In Portland, I've enjoyed being a sideman and accompanist playing with many of Portland's best musicians: singers Rebecca Kilgore and Nancy King, saxophonist David Evans, and cornetist Jim Goodwin (now deceased) to name a few. For the past thirty years, twenty-three of them with my wife, April Magnusson, Portland has been my home.

Acknowledgments

This book would never have existed without my experiences and friend-ships with my fellow musicians and members of the jazz community. I especially want to thank my many friends and colleagues who read this book in its early versions and the following individuals who assisted me with getting it published: Neal McCabe, for his organizational advice when I started writing. David Rosner, my music publisher, a close friend, and my champion from back when I began to write songs, who steered me to Backbeat Books, where John Cerullo found my book appropriate for publishing. Edward Sorel, for his generosity in allow-ing me use of his artwork for the book cover. Special thanks to Lindsay Wagner, who kept this project on course; Polly Watson, for her gentle and thorough editing; and all the other folks at Backbeat Books who helped. Last, but not least, thanks to Jay Schornstein, my friend and attorney, and to April Magnusson, my loving and patient wife, both of whom spent many days keeping me calm and helping me organize, edit, and prepare *My Dear Departed Past*.

Index

Abdul-Malik, Ahmed, 86

Adelman, Leo, 10

Alexander, Mousey, 97

Aliferis, James, 22

Allen, Dr. George, 28

Allen Park Drive and Bird
    Sanctuary, 28

Allison, Mose, 98, 102

Alpert, Herb, 31

American Society of Motion
    Picture Arrangers and
    Composers (ASMAC), 107

Ammons, Albert, 8

Amos, John, 124

Annen, Honest John, 100

Apartment the (club), 144

April, Kerri, 52

April Music, 120

Arlen, Harold, 69–70, 143

Armstrong, Louis, 19, 86

Avery, Ray, 70

Bacharach, Burt, 59, 120

Bailey, Mildred, 7

Bargy, Jeanne, 46

Barksdale, Everett, 133

Barra, 140–42

Bartell, Dick, 94,

Bartók, Béla, 23–25, 111

Baseball Digest, xii, 9

Baseball Magazine, 185

Basin Street East, 93

Baxter, Glenn, 18,

Beal, John, 57, 63

Bechet, Sidney, 9

Beiderbecke, Bix, 73, 89,
    149–151

Benchley, Robert, 7

Benson, George, 25

Benson, Sumner, 15

Bergman, Alan, 62

Bergman, Marilyn, 62

Berlinger, Warren, 124

Bernhart, Milt, 107

Berry, Jack, 107–110

Best, Denzil, 91

beatnik, 87–88, 98

Bell Sound, 133

Bicycle Music, 80

Bigard, Barney, 19

Birnberg, Ted, 14

Blakkestad, Bill, 20

Blanton, Jimmy, 92

Blaupunkt, 60

Bluebird, 7

Bob Ochs Combo, 15–16

Bonoff, Ed, 44

Boone, Pat, 65

Braff, Ruby, 85–86

Bravo, Jaime, 143

Broadbent, Alan, 19

Broderick, James, 122

Broun, Heywood, 177, 179

Brown, Lawrence, 19

Brown, Marshall, 85–87

Brown, Sam, 63

Brunswick, 9

Bunch, John, 85

Burns, Roy, 82

Café au Go Go, 91

Cain, Jackie, 19

Calabrese, Bucky, 73

Calloway, Cab, 7

Candoli, Conte, 19

Canterino, Frank, 93

Canterino, Mike, 93, 97

Canterino, Sonny, 93, 97

Carle, Frankie, 7, 102

Carlin, George, 91

Carmichael, Hoagy, 73,
    150–152

Catholic Charities, 38

Cavett, Dick, 173, 175

Central High School, 9, 14

Chaloff, Serge, 19

Charles, Keith, 47

Charles, Ray, 59, 123

Charlton, Jim, 170–175

Charlie's Tavern, 48

Chevy Bel Air, 28, 34

Christopher, Chet, 14

Cicotte, Eddie, 182–183

Cinderella Club, 86

Claire, Dick, 124

Clayton, Buck, 112

Club Carnival, 19

Coan, Jack, 18, 20

Cochran, Charlie, 71

Cohn, Al, 19, 22, 93, 95–102, 113

Coleman, Ornette, 68

Coller, Tom, 15–16

Collins, John, 20

Collins, Joyce, 144

Coltrane, John, 68, 110

Columbia Records, 10–11, 51, 103

Concord Records, 122

Condon, Eddie, 65–66, 69, 142, 144

Congressional Medal of Honor, 26

Cook, Barbara, 132

Copland, Aaron, 21, 25

Cordy, Henry, 36, 41

Corwin, Bob, 142–143

Cottrell, Jack, 18

Coward, Noël, 52–53, 66

Craft, Robert, 64–65

Crea, Bob, 14, 19–20

Crosby, Bing, 7

Crothers, Scatman, 27

Crow, Bill, 82

Davern, Kenny, 65

David, Hal, 62

Davis, Art, 91

Davis, Bob, 20

Davis, Lockjaw, 93

Davis, Richard, 90–91

Davison, Wild Bill, 10, 86

Dearie, Blossom, 63, 79–81, 102, 119, 144

DeBenedictis, Dick, 85

Decca, 2, 7, 103

DeForest, Charles, 144

Denoff, Sam, 37–39, 41–43, 123, 128

Desmond, Paul, 111

Dexamyl, 35, 49, 64

Dexedrine, 49, 64

Dial, 10

Diamante's, 144

Dick Van Dyke Show, The, 38, 123

Dillon, Red, 145–146

Dodgion, Jerry, 82

Domanico, Chuck, 137

Donovan, Bobby, 56, 73

Donte's, 74, 131, 140, 145–146

Dorham, Kenny, 90

Dorough, Bob, 19, 62–63, 119, 131, 156–158
Down Beat, viii, xii, 9
Drew, Kenny, 50
Duplex, the, 44–46, 48

Eastman, John, 119
Eckstine, Billy, 15
Edwards, Teddy, 157
Ellington, Duke, 5, 92–93 102–103, 166, 172
Elliot Lawrence Band, 17
Elliott, Jack, 72, 123, 127–128
Evans, David, 193

Fantasy Records, 121
FAO Schwarz, 64
Fat Tuesday's, 113
Feather, Lorraine, 62
Feingold, Jay, 83
Ferguson, Allyn, 123, 126, 128
Fichera, Chris, 121
Finch, Dee, 36–38
Fine, Elliot, 17
Fine, Jack, 86–87
Finley, Pat, 124
Finley, Paul, 15
Fischer, Clare, 137–138
Fiske, Dwight, 52

Fitzgerald, Ella, 7, 19
Fitzgerald, Pat, 14
Flame, the, 19–20
Flower Drum Song, 45
Ford, Art, 36
Fort Douglas, 25, 28
Foster, Al, 90
Foster, Gary, 137
Frank, Leonard (Zeke), 132–133
Frank Music, 77, 79, 118–119
Frazier, Oscar, 14
Free, Ronnie, 63
Freeman, Bud, 9, 65–70, 89
Freeman, Russ, 82

Gaîeté Parisienne, 17
Gandil, Chick, 188
Gardner, Ava, 65
Garland, Judy, 71–72
Garner, Erroll, 102
Gate of Horn, 147
Gaylor, Hal, 48–49
Gaynor, Mitzi, 85
Getz, Stan, 13, 29, 95, 166
Gilbert and Sullivan, 7
Gillespie, Dizzy, 9–10
Gillman, Harold, 14–15
Gilmore, Steve, 121
Goldfus, Shelly, 18

Goldkette, Jean, 43

Golly, Cecil, 17–18

Gonsalves, Paul, 93

Goodman, Benny, 7, 25, 82–86

Goodman, Miles, 134

Goodwin, Bill, 121, 157

Goodwin, Jim, 193

Gorsica, Johnny, 94

Graham, Stella (formerly Gianmasi), 47, 132

Grauer, Irving, 57

Graves, Teresa, 124

Great American Music Hall, 121

Great Northern Hotel, 69

Greenberg, Ruth, 123

Greenwell, Fred, 63, 82

Greenwillow, 47

Greer, Sonny, 19

Grossman, Albert, 62

Groveland Park Elementary School, xi

Gurney Jr., A. R., 122

Guryan, Margo, 120

Guthrie, Woody, 8

Haggart, Bob, 69–70

Half Note, the, 61, 71–72, 74, 91–93, 95–100

Hall, Kiki, 52–54

Hammond, John, 78

Hanna, Jake, 95

Haymes, Bob, 41

Haymes, Dick, 73

Heidt, Horace, 7

Henderson, Joe, 90

Herman, Woody, 15, 29, 103

Hester, Carolyn, 61

Heywood, Eddie, 102

Hill AFB, 34

Hines, Earl, 19

Hodges, Johnny, 19, 93

Hofstra College, 38

Hogsett, Elon, 94

Holiday, Billie, 19

Hollenden Hotel, 68

Holley, Major, 98

Hood, Bill, 137, 139

Hoop-de-Doo, the, 20–21

Hotel Sutton, 144

Hotel Theresa, 94, 145–146

Houston, Cisco, 8

Howard's Steakhouse, 14

Howe, Jackie, 52–54

Huffsteter, Steve, 137, 139

Hughart, Ted, 18, 20

Hymie's Bar, 65

Iooss, Walter, 41

Jeffries, Fran, 73, 77

Jennings, Hughie, 185

Jensen, Bob, 15

Jerome, Jerome K., 89

Jobson, King, 15

Johnson, James P., 92

Johnson, J. J., 133

Johnson, Osie, 133

Johnson, Pete, 8, 102, 132

Jolly Miller Room, 17–18

Jones, Elvin, 91

Jones, Philly Joe, 91

Jordan, Sheila, 53–54

Kamuca, Richie, 93

Kaplan, Shirley, 14

Karlin, Fred, 78

Karr, Dave, 18–20

Katz, Leon, 14

Kawai, 46

Kellaway, Roger, 113

Kelly, Gene, 124, 127

Kent, Bubbles, 52, 54

Kenton, Stan, 9

Kern, Jerome, 47

Kilgore, Rebecca, 193

King, Nancy, 193

Klavan and Finch, 37

Klavan, Gene, 36, 38–39

Knapp, Johnny, 51, 57, 59

Kohn, Dick, 14

Komischke, Ray, 14

Kral, Irene, 144

Kral, Roy, 19

Krall, Diana, 79

Kramer, Milt, 77–78

Krupa, Gene, 83–84, 87–88

Kunin, Bob, 19–20

Kyser, Kay, 7

Lackland Air Force Base, 30

Lamond, Don, 69

Landesman, Fran, 62

Lang, Eddie, 73

Lanin, Lester, 74

Lapof, Ray, 35–36

Leadbelly, 8, 62

Lee, Peggy, 13, 81, 103

Leeman, Cliff, 65

Leifman, Mel, 20

Leigh, Carolyn, 62

Lembeck, Michael, 124

Leonard, Sheldon, 38

Le Ruban Bleu, 47

Levy, Lou, 19–20

Lewis, Meade Lux, 8, 132

Lewis, Mel, 90–92, 94

Ley, Willy, 39

Limbaugh, Rush, 115

Lincoln Center for the
   Performing Arts, 122
LiPuma, Tommy, 79–80
Little, Steve, 73
Loesser, Frank, 47, 77
L.A. Philharmonic, 25
Louise's Music Store, 9
Lovett, Lyle, 80
Lucas, Al, 112
Lutes, Marcy, 50

Ma, Yo-Yo, 166
Macalester College, 62
MacMillan *Baseball
   Encyclopedia*, 171
Magnusson, April, 193, 195
Mandel, Johnny, 150–151,
   190–191
Manne, Shelly, 137–138
Margolis, Sam, 66
Mark, Maurice, 56, 74, 113
Mark Taper Forum, 151
Marshall High School, 15
Marshall, Wendell, 133
Martin, Stu (Stewie), 49–50
Marx, Chico, 102
Mathews, Mat, 133
Mathewson, Christy, 177–179,
   182, 185–188
Mayflower Hotel, 37

McBroom, Amanda, 152
McCabe, Neal, 62, 195
McCaffrey, Bob, 20,
McCurdy, Roy, 140
McKenna, Dave, 63
McKinney, Ray, 90
McMahon, Jenna, 124
McManus, Al, 86
McPartland, Jimmy, 9
McRae, Carmen, 132
Mercer, Amanda, 142–143
Mercer, Johnny, 70, 72,
   142–145
Messner, Johnny, 48
Metronome, xii, 9
Metropole, the, 53, 61, 83–84,
   87
Meyerding, Charles, 15
Mezzrow, Mezz, 9
Michael, Major Edward, 26,
   34
Midway Gardens, 17
Mikrokosmos, 23
Milkman's Matinee, 36
Minneapolis Roosevelt High,
   15
Minneapolis Symphony
   Orchestra, 14, 23
Mister George, 100
Mitchell, Adrian, 151–152

Monk, Thelonious, 53, 68, 102, 111

Montalbán, Carlos, 143

Montowese Playhouse, 48

Montowese resort hotel, 47

Moore, Hal, 42

Moore, Russ, 20

Moran and Mack, 80

Morton, Jelly Roll, 8

Mountain Sound, 121

Muhammad, Elijah, 94

Mulcrone, Jimmy, 11–12, 14

Mulligan, Gerry, 17

Muranyi, Joe, 86

Music by Golly, 17

Musicians' Local 802, 55

Mustin, Burt, 124

Nance, Ray, 50, 90

National Pastime, the, 167, 170–171

Nelson, Norm, 14, 20

Nevis, MN, 16

Newall, George, 157–158

Newsom, Tommy, 82, 85

Nicholas, Big Nick, 133

Nichols, Herbie, 53–54

Nick's Tavern, 65

Nicollet Hotel, 17

Nola Rehearsal Studio, 47

Northwestern College of Chiropractic, 15

O'Brien, Kenny, 87

Ochs, Bob, 15–16

O'Day, Anita, 71, 73–74

Okeh, 7

Olin, Jimmy, 52

Oliver, Lynn, 90

Omni Sound, 121–122

Owen, Marvin, 94

Page Three, the, 51, 53–55

Paris Hotel, 35

Park Rapids, MN, 16

Parker, Charlie, 10, 14, 29, 101, 111

Pasquale's, 140

Paymar, Jerry, 14

Perlman, Dave, 87

Perlman, Itzhak, 166

Persky, Bill, 37–38, 41–43, 123, 127–128

Pettiford, Ira, 14

Pheasant Gazette, the, 28–29

Pincus, Bob, 35–36

Pizza on the Park, 114

Plapinger, Bobby, 187–188

Point Mugu naval observatory, 142

Pointer, Priscilla, 122

Poole, John, 71

Powell, Bud, 102, 111

Powell, Mel, 8, 82, 103

Previn, André, 166

Price, Nikki, 78

Queen, Ellery, 7

Rank, Bill, 73

Rath, Dick, 44

RCA Victor Records, 42

Reach *Baseball Guide*, 185

Red Cross, the, 38

Red Rodney, 10

Redding, Otis, 59

Reid, Rufus, 113

Reiner, Carl, 38

Renzi, Mike, 191

Reserve Officers' Training
    Corps, xii

Richardson, Jerome, 133

Rick's Cafe Americain, 146–147

Riverboat Room, 74

Robin, Leo, 144

Rockler, Sheldon, 14

Roker, Mickey, 91

Rollini, Adrian, 73

Rollins, Sonny, 111

Roseland Ballroom, 55

Rosner, Ben, 43, 45

Rosner, David, 79–80, 116,
    118–120, 195

Rosolino, Frank, 85

Ross, Roy, 41

Rowles, Jimmy, 13, 92,
    102–103, 137

Roycraft Company, 10

R. Plapinger Baseball Books,
    187

Rubenstein, Billy, 44,
    47–48

Rumplemayer's, 35

Runyon, Damon, 179

Rushing, Jimmy, 96

St. Thomas Academy, 15

Samuel, Gerard, 24

Sargent, Rick, 47

Sauter, Eddie, 82

Sayers, Dorothy, 7

Scharf, Stuart, 157

Schmitt Music, 11, 132

Schoolhouse Rock, 131,
    153–161

Scott, Raymond, 7

Senatore, Pat, 140

Severinson, Doc, 131

Shadur, Bob, 14

Shalimar, the, 89–94

Shapiro, George, 127

Shaw, Artie, 7

Sheen, Mickey, 67–68

Sheldon, Jack, 74, 85, 157

Showboat, the, 48

Siegelson, Bert, 77–78

Silver, Horace, 13

Simon, Ron, xi

Sims, Zoot, 19, 82, 93,
    95–99, 101–102, 113

Sinton Hotel, 179

Six Fat Dutchmen, the, 99

Six, Jack, 65

Sky, Pat, 61

Smith, Pine Top, 8

Smith, Queenie, 124

Smith, W. Eugene, 63

Society for American Baseball
    Research, 170

Spanier, Muggsy, 9–10

Specht, Don, 14, 19–20

Spicer, Myles, 14

Sporting News, the, xii, 9

Sports Collectors Digest, 187

Stacy, Jess, 8, 147

Stanford University, 18

Starr, Lonnie, 37

Stewart, Slam, 20,

Stone, Radford, 157

Stravinsky, Igor, 64–65, 98, 150

Strayhorn, Billy, 93

Studd, Tony, 48

Studebaker, 14

Sudhalter, Dick, 151

Sullivan, Billy, 94

Sullivan, Ed, 41

Sullivan, Dan, 122

Suzuki, Pat, 45

Swallow, Steve, 67–68

Takas, Bill, 59–60, 63, 87

Talley, Maurice, 14

T & R Studio, 137

Tate, Buddy, 112

Tate Gallery, 5

Tate, Grady, 91, 158

Tatum, Art, 8, 20, 92

Taylor, Cecil, 54–55

Taylor, Montana, 132

Tedesco, Tommy, 135

Terry, Clark, 133

Teschemacher, Frank, 9

Theatrical Lounge, 67

Thompson, Dick, 5, 18, 20

Thornhill, Claude, 102

Three Peters, 119–120

Thurber, James, 7

Tiny Tim, 52–55

Tjornhom, Tom, 15

Tompkins, Ross, 48, 113

Tormé, Mel, 72

Tough, Dave, 89

Trader Jon's, 48, 50

Trestman, Jerry, 14

Triffon, George, 73

Trumbauer, Frankie, 73

Uhry, Alfred, 77, 143

Union Army, 25

Unique Monique, the, 53–54

United Negro College Fund, the, 38

U.S., 79

U.S. Coast Guard, 38

University of Minnesota, xii, 8, 18, 21

Upin, Joel, 60

Van Ronk, Dave, 61

Ventura, Charlie, 9, 16, 19, 87

Vic and Sade, 7

Vic's, 19

Village Vanguard, the, 51, 91

Villars, Conway, 15, 17

Vine Street Bar and Grill, 121

Vinnegar, Leroy, 157

Vivian Beaumont Theater, 122, 128

Vocalion, 7

Von Braun, Wernher, 39

Waldman, Bob, 77

Waldorf, Jack, 83

Walken, Christopher, 122

Walker, MN, 16–17

Waller, Fats, 92

Warren, Adrian, 14

Warrick, Ruth, 191

Warwick, Dionne, 59

Washington, DC, 48

Washington Square Bar and Grill, 119

Wasserman, Eddie, 87

Watson, Laurel, 52

WDGY Barn Dance, 18

Webster, Ben, 4, 89–95, 145–146

Wechter, Julius, 31

West, George, 48

West, Mae, 80

Wettling, George, 86

White, Josh, 8

Whiteman, Paul, 73, 150

Whoopee John, 99

Williams, Chuck, 15

Williams, Cindy, 124

Williams, Jackie, 91, 112

Williams, Paul, 62

Williams, William B., 36–37

Willson, Meredith, 142

Wilson, Teddy, 8

Winding, Kai, 45, 47–48, 50, 107

Winters, Pinky, 25

WNEW, 34, 36–37, 40–41, 43, 123

Wodehouse, P. G., 66, 89

Woods, Phil, 95

World War II, 7, 27

Yaged, Sol, 53, 84

Yancey, Jimmy, 8

Yankovic, Frankie, 99

Yohe, Tom, 157

Young, David X., 44, 95

Young, Lester, 66, 101, 105

Zawinul, Joe, 92

Zeiler, Sid, 57–59

Zemlin, Dick, 18